Emily Post's
Everyday Etiquette

Emily Post's
Everyday Etiquette

HOW TO HANDLE THE TOP
MANNERS DILEMMAS

Peggy Post

EMILY POST'S EVERYDAY ETIQUETTE

Emily Post is a registered trademark of
The Emily Post Institute, Inc.

This 2013 edition published by Barnes & Noble, Inc. by
arrangement with HarperCollins Publishers.

Barnes & Noble, Inc.
122 Fifth Avenue
New York, NY 10011

ISBN: 978-1-4351-4585-6

Printed and bound in the United States of America.

13 14 15 16 17 LPX / RRD 5 4 3 2 1

CONTENTS

What Do I Do If…?
Questions, questions, questions!

For some people, both the name Emily Post and the idea of etiquette may seem out of touch, what with the pace, technologies, and sophistication of our lives. But the truth is that The Emily Post Institute receives more and more questions about manners every day—in fact, thousands of questions every month. The questions come to us through many channels: our website, www.emilypost.com; our editorial partners (among them *Good Housekeeping, The New York Times, The Boston Globe* and *Inside Weddings*); the business etiquette seminars and children's manners workshops that we teach; book tours and the hundreds of personal appearances we make each year. The deluge also comes from the media—print, radio, television and online reporters. These Emily questions keep us up-to-date about what's on people's minds, and we are delighted to help them people find the answers for navigating tricky situations.

The topics in this book cover both the traditional and the modern situations in contemporary life—from same-sex weddings to long-established wedding rituals; from bilingual discussions in office-place cubicles to a co-worker's body odor; from making an introduction when you can't remember someone's name to responding to nosy questions about your salary; from when to take a hostess gift to whether to apply lipstick at the table—and far beyond.

These are times when people seek "scripts" for life's dilemmas, a book to look to for a simple answer to a complex relationship quandary. *Emily Post on Etiquette: How to Handle the Top Manners Dilemmas* offers clear solutions for life's potentially awkward moments. If you're trying to figure out whether you can bring a date to your best friend's wedding without asking the hosts if that's okay—your answer is here. Unsure how to tip when your service is horrible? No problem. Want someone to back you up when you say you don't need to respond to an RSVP? That's something we don't do, but if you're wondering about how to deal with the mother who can't control her pestering toddler on the airplane, look here for advice on what to say. This book also contains tips for unfriending a friend on Facebook—and much more.

Consider *Emily Post on Etiquette* as your go-to guide. It has a wealth of information gathered in one place to make life's everyday uncertainties a little easier to sort out. After all, as Emily Post said, "When people come together, you have etiquette." On any given day, it's quite possible to run into dozens of situations in which it's a matter of asking oneself "what to do?" Herein, many of our most frequently asked questions—and answers for how to deal with them. These tips may not cover everything, but I hope they'll get you out of more than a few jams—and guide you through some of life's most important moments.

Sincerely,

PEGGY POST
SUMMER 2013

1

Conversations:

The Good, the Bad, and the Awkward

Smooth-Talking Tips

QUESTION: My wife's company is holding a holiday party next week and I'm the world's worst conversationalist. Any advice?

ANSWER: Take heart—most conversational blunders are committed by those who talk too much, not too little. Think before you speak. Have a list of possible topics in mind that will help get a conversation going. Avoid yes or no questions. "What are your plans for the holidays?" will take you further than "Are you traveling for the holidays?" Don't be afraid to introduce yourself, especially to another outsider, who may feel like a fish out of water, too.

THE FINE ART OF SMALL TALK

Some people just seem to have the gift of gab—they can chat up even virtual strangers with ease. Here's how to become a great conversationalist:

1. **BE WELL VERSED ON CURRENT EVENTS.** Make it your mission to be a generalist. Read local and national newspapers and news magazines and watch TV news shows to bone up on events in your town and around the nation and world. Keep up on entertainment

and the arts with general-interest magazines and TV. Know which sports teams are winning and which aren't.

2. **ASK PEOPLE FOR THEIR OPINIONS.** Before you go to an event, think of a few questions you can ask at the start of a conversation. People usually love to be asked for their views on a subject.

3. **STEER CLEAR OF CONTROVERSIAL TOPICS**. Politics, sex, and religion are potential minefields. You want to start a pleasant conversation, not an argument.

4. **KNOW YOUR HOSTS**. If you don't already know much about your hosts, learn their interests ahead of time. Are they into skiing, hiking, travel, computers? You can ask around, or check out pictures and other objects on display in your hosts' home for clues. Whether you are chatting with them or fellow guests, the hosts' interests can jump-start a conversation.

5. **PRACTICE, PRACTICE, PRACTICE.** The people you meet every day—taxicab drivers, store clerks, UPS delivery personnel—can be conversation partners, too. The more you practice, the easier it gets.

6. **REMEMBER TO LISTEN.** Put aside your worries about what to say next, and instead concentrate on what the other person is saying. He'll enjoy chatting with you much more if you're actively listening (that means eye contact and an occasional nod or brief comment). Plus, the conversation will flow back and forth more easily for you, since you'll be able to branch out from what he's just said. If you're truly at a loss, ask him a question and listen some more.

✵

Top Ten Nosy Questions—
and Quick Retorts

1. "HOW MUCH MONEY DO YOU MAKE?"

"Not enough to buy the house that's going up down the road."

"My mother told me never to discuss money, except with my accountant."

2. "DID YOU MAKE A KILLING WHEN YOU SOLD YOUR HOUSE?"

"We did just fine, thanks."

3. "HOW MUCH DID YOU PAY FOR THAT SUIT?"

"Why, does it look expensive?"

4. "IS YOUR CHILD ADOPTED?"

"He really does have his own unique personality, doesn't he?"

5. "DO YOU DYE YOUR HAIR?"

"Sorry, that's between me and my hairstylist."

6. "HAVE YOU HAD WORK DONE—LIKE A FACE-LIFT?"

"Hey, do I look younger? It must be all that clean living!"

7. "WHY ARE YOU GOING TO THE DOCTOR?"

"You don't want to know."

8. "ARE YOU FEELING OKAY? YOU LOOK TIRED."
   "Actually, I feel great!"

9. "HOW OLD ARE YOU?"
   "Twenty-nine and holding."
   "Today I feel about 93."

10. "WHAT ARE YOU TWO TALKING ABOUT?"
   "Nothing to write home about."

RESPONSE RESCUES

Use humor. Make a light joke out of the question.

Use body language. Let your facial expression say, "Don't go there."

Tell it like it is. "I'd rather not say," or, "I'm not comfortable answering that question."

"Back atcha." When all else fails, turn the tables with this one-size-fits-all response to a nosy question: "Why do you ask?"

�֍

Recovering From Foot-in-Mouth Disease

QUESTION: I recently asked the librarian at my daughter's school when her baby was due. To my horror, she responded, "I'm not pregnant." I could only manage to stutter, "Oh, I'm so sorry!" and disappear as soon as I could. What should I have done?

ANSWER: Don't be too hard on yourself; how you responded was just fine. The best recovery is to apologize and change the subject—fast. "Sorry! My eyes must be going! Speaking of which, I like your new glasses. Where did you get them?"

FINESSING THE FLUB

The Flub: Mistaking a friend's sister for her mother.
Finesse It: "I thought Stacy told me she was meeting her mother for lunch today. Well, you do look way too young to be Stacy's mother!" Most people are more than willing to overlook a comment that was not intended to be hurtful.

The Flub: Your young son points to a man at the grocery store and yells, "Look at his big, fat belly, Mommy!"

Finesse It: Ah, the candor of children! Calmly tell your son to quiet down and then apologize for him to the other shopper. Later, explain to your child that he shouldn't say things that hurt other people's feelings.

The Flub: Complaining about having to find a Mother's Day present to a friend who recently lost her mother.

Finesse It: Fess up to being an insensitive dolt—"I'm sorry. I wasn't thinking"—and then move on.

The Flub: Saying, "It's nice to meet you," at a business meeting and having the person reply, "Don't you remember? We met last month at the Chamber Convention."

Finesse It: "I remember. I'm just so bad at names. Sorry!" If you can, add something that shows you aren't totally forgetful: "We talked about the new software your company is developing for hospital administrators." This shows that at least you remember the conversation. Here's a helpful tip: When you're introduced to someone you may have met before, say "It's nice to see you" instead of "It's nice to meet you."

✺

Party Politics

QUESTION: At a party recently, I started talking politics with some of the guests and the discussion got heated. The host seemed uncomfortable. I enjoy a good debate and think our argument was civil, but my wife insists it was rude to talk politics at a party. Who's right?

ANSWER: An intelligent discussion of an interesting topic can be great party entertainment, provided no one curses or resorts to full-scale arguing. Most subjects—world events, sports, the stock market, even war and politics—are fair game if everyone expresses himself rationally, listens with an open mind, and refrains from insisting too vehemently on his own views. Unless your conversation amounted to all-out verbal combat, it shouldn't be considered rude.

THE THREE RULES OF ENGAGEMENT

Although it's okay to broach potentially sensitive topics at social gatherings, it's important to do it in a way that will stimulate intelligent discussion—not get anyone's back up or start a brawl. Here's how to keep the discussion civil:

1. *Consider Your Audience*

Think twice before introducing a hot-button subject. If someone in the room has a family member in the military, for example, starting a discussion about the war on terror is not a great idea.

2. *Don't Attack*

Saying "You're wrong!" or "That's not true!" is like saying your conversation partner is less than intelligent or less than honest. It's more tactful to say, "I don't think I agree with you about that," or, "It seems to me . . ."

3. *Know How to End It*

If an argument is going nowhere, put a stop to it and clear the air with a comment like, "Poor Catherine, I bet she didn't expect fireworks when she invited us over." Or, "Harry, I've enjoyed our debate as much as Catherine's wonderful dinner. But let's say we now drop the subject and simply agree to disagree. Okay?" Or, "Well, we obviously don't agree on this one, but I can see your point of view." And then, by all means, change the subject: "How about them Yankees?"

✳

Cutting Ties With
Your Hairdresser

QUESTION: I just got a great haircut from another stylist at my regular salon when my stylist was out sick. I'd love to switch to the new hairdresser, but my current stylist has cut my hair for the last four years and I don't want to hurt her feelings. Help!

ANSWER: Breaking up with a hairdresser is like ending any relationship: The key is to be honest and polite. Avoiding the situation could cause hurt feelings. Instead, talk to your old stylist. Tell her that her coworker has taken your hair in a new direction: "I really liked the way Pam cut my hair, so I'm going to make my next appointment with her. I hope you understand." Thank her and offer to refer friends to her. Hopefully, she will understand and also appreciate the fact that you're keeping your business at the salon. You may feel awkward, but it's a situation that most stylists have encountered. In fact, the consensus among stylists and other professionals is that they prefer to know the reason why someone leaves them. They want their clients to be happy, so they welcome feedback.

FIRING FAIRLY: THE POLITE ADIEU

It's not easy firing your stylist, babysitter, housecleaner, or assistant. In fact, many people say they'd rather put up with the spiked haircut or the dust bunnies under the chairs than let someone go. They're not wimps. It's just that they don't like to hurt others' feelings. But sometimes it's necessary to bid adieu, and there's a right way to do it.

- *Have a good reason.* As a client or an employer, you're responsible for communicating the job description and your expectations. Outline what you want from the very beginning, and update your preferences as necessary.

- *Give fair warning.* Many firings occur due to general incompetence or a specific slacking off. Before firing, give the employee or service provider a warning—a reasonable presentation of your concern—and also give him or her a chance to correct the problem.

- *Give adequate notice.* Sometimes, the problem is not due to performance. Instead, the services are no longer needed or feasible. Your situation could change: Perhaps you're becoming an empty-nest parent without the need for regular housecleaning, or your budget no longer enables you to splurge at the deluxe salon. Explain as soon as you can.

- *Be honest.* This means no made-up reasons. Don't pretend that you're giving up having a housecleaner entirely, only to turn around and hire someone else. Instead, tell the person you're letting go that things didn't improve after you pointed out specific problems. Now, it's time to move on.

- *Be kind.* There's no need to be cruel. There's always something good to say about the person and the work that has been performed.

❉

Handicapped Parking Dilemma

QUESTION: I have a license plate with a handicapped symbol and use the handicapped spaces when I park. But I sometimes get dirty looks and rude comments from people because they can't see my disability. How should I respond?

ANSWER: Because your disability isn't visible, some people may wrongly assume you're abusing the privilege of handicapped parking. The safe response is to do nothing and ignore the looks and comments. Although this may hurt your pride and may not stop the negative reactions, responding could make the situation escalate into a nasty confrontation. If you want to respond, stand your ground with grace. In a calm, pleasant voice, say, "You look upset. Is something wrong?" Think Mother Teresa, not Tony Soprano. If you speak politely, you may be able to start a conversation about it without the situation getting testy. Or, try an ounce of prevention: Print up some cards to display on your dashboard with a message that says something like this: "I have debilitating arthritis. While I may look okay to you, the short walk from my car to the store is a major challenge for me. That's why I have handicapped parking access." Of course, some incorrigible characters couldn't care less what your ailment is. They are incapable of empathy, so just ignore them.

HOW TO TREAT A PERSON WITH A DISABILITY

People with disabilities number about seventeen percent of the United States population, which is a large minority group. The humanity of these fifty million individuals is no different from yours. Focusing on this fact should make it easier for you to put aside any anxiety and be yourself when you interact with a person who has a disability.

- Don't stare, even discreetly.
- All basic manners apply—friendly greetings, smiles, "please" and "thank you," and introductions.
- Avoid being overly solicitous. If you want to help, ask first. People who have mastered getting about in wheelchairs, on crutches, or in braces, or who manage without the benefit of vision or hearing, take justifiable pride in their independence. Take your cue from the person with the special needs or from his caregiver.
- Refrain from asking personal questions of a person with a disability. If he wants to talk about the condition, he'll broach the subject.
- Don't pity the person. Life is what you make it. If a person with a disability doesn't see his life as tragic, then it most certainly isn't.

❆

2

How Rude!

Rude Awakening

QUESTION: When I had to return something at a clothing store recently, the salesperson kept me waiting a long time and then was very curt—she didn't apologize or say "Thank you," "Have a nice day," or even "Good-bye." How should I respond when an employee is rude?

ANSWER: You have a choice: Speak up or say nothing. If you want to respond, look the person in the eye, smile, and say, "Thanks!" Overwhelmed or underpaid, anyone can have a bad day; a positive encounter could change the karma. If not, you might let the management know that someone on their sales staff is forgetting basic courtesies. Even better, write a letter—with specifics. Complaints in writing are harder to ignore.

"EXCUSE ME, YOU'RE RUDE!"

Most people simply ignore rudeness, perhaps because they're afraid a minor quarrel could escalate or because an affront happens so quickly, they don't have a chance to react. It's okay to stand up to rude behavior as long as you don't respond in kind or sense that a nasty confrontation could erupt. Staying cool and pleasant is the best way to make your point. There might even be a bonus: Perhaps your good manners will be contagious. Here are some guidelines for deciding whether to respond to rude behavior—or not:

Don't take it personally. Perhaps the offender is having a bad day. Take the focus off your hurt feelings by imagining what he might be going through—the sting of a recent confrontation, financial troubles, an ill spouse.

Size up your annoyances. Will it accomplish anything to make a stink about the person who's using a credit card at the "Cash Only" register, or will it just be a waste of your emotional energy?

Set a good example. Rudeness begets rudeness. If you speak sharply to a bank teller, don't be surprised if you get the same treatment in return.

Count to ten. When someone's behavior makes you angry, take a few deep breaths and ask yourself, "Is it really worth blowing my stack over this?"

Laugh it off. Countering the comment "You look awful!" with a sarcastic retort like "How kind of you to say so!" is preferable to "Well, you don't look so hot yourself!" If you can't come up with a friendly joke, just chuckle and change the subject.

✳

Telephone Troubles

QUESTION: I've left several messages for the public information officer at a local nonprofit where I'm working on a fund-raiser. She hasn't returned my phone calls. What should I do?

ANSWER: Try once more before giving up. Say, "Mrs. Hollings, this is Jack Pierce (at phone number xxx). I'm the Kids' Day Committee member calling about the April event. I'm worried about meeting the fund-raising committee's deadlines, so could you please give me a call? I need information from you before moving forward. Thanks." Be sure to leave your number. If there is still no response, contact someone else at the organization and politely explain the problem and ask for help. Or, if you can get the information elsewhere, by all means, do.

THE RUDEST OF TIMES

As the pace of modern life speeds up, rudeness seems to escalate, too. Below are some of the most offensive and, sadly, most common rude behaviors of our day:

Doing the "cell yell." Broadcasting a cell phone conversation in a public place as if your phone mate were hard of hearing.

Driving recklessly. Zipping from lane to lane (without signaling, unfortunately) and generally driving like a maniac, endangering the lives of others.

Telling racist or ethnic jokes. Passing along unfunny "jokes" that insult the listener's intelligence while smearing entire races and populations.

Looking down on servers and sales help. Treating workers rudely or as if they were somehow beneath you.

Swearing in public. Using obscenities or four-letter words, which are especially offensive when children are within earshot.

Allowing your kids to bother others. Letting kids run wild or make noise in restaurants, supermarkets, theaters, or any other public or private place.

Abusing the umpire. Just because the ref/coach/umpire makes a call that doesn't work in your child's or team's favor doesn't mean it's okay to harass the sports official or the opposing team's players or spectators.

Leaving a mess on the sidewalk. Fouling the walkway or street with spit, trash, or pet poop left unscooped.

Not giving up your seat. On public transportation, staying planted in your seat when an elderly, pregnant, or person with a disability obviously needs it more than you do.

Charging through crowds. This is especially obnoxious—and dangerous—when the charger is skating, riding a bike or an electric scooter, or pushing a baby stroller. Even minus the extra equipment, anyone who pushes though crowds—especially without so much as an "Excuse me!"—is just plain rude.

Cutting in. Doing so on a checkout line, or taking a parking space that someone else is clearly waiting for.

Holding up the checkout line while cell-phoning or texting. Ignoring others—wasting their time while you're on your cell phone.

"Excuse Me, But I Was Next"

QUESTION: Recently, I was in a long line at the grocery store and had been waiting quite a while. A new lane opened up and a woman who had just joined the end of the line rushed over to get there first. The cashier started ringing up her purchases. What should I have done?

ANSWER: If someone jumps in front of you in line, you can immediately say, "Excuse me, but I was ahead of you. I believe I'm next." If the person doesn't retreat, don't push it—just go speak to the manager. Suggest that when a cashier opens a new register, he should say "May I help the next person in line?" Then next time, see if the request is followed correctly.

THE RIGHT RESPONSE

When someone's behavior irks you, ask yourself if it's worthwhile to take on the person who's acting rudely. The answer is usually no. But even if you decide to keep mum, there is one subtle but effective antidote to rudeness: Kill 'em with kindness. At the very least, you may shame the offender into acting more civilized. Here are a few other strategies for dealing with rudeness:

Give the offender the benefit of the doubt. Try not to take the rudeness personally.

Offer empathy. If a young child behind you on a plane is kicking your seat, calmly say to the parent, "I know space is tight and kids have lots of energy, but your son has been kicking my seat since we boarded. I'd appreciate it if you'd ask him to stop. Thanks!" Or, if it's an older child or an adult, make the same calm request directly.

Encourage a positive response. "Shut up! You're driving me crazy!" is not going to get the results you're looking for. Instead, try "A few of us are trying to read. Could you please lower your voice? Thanks!" Say it with a smile.

Take it to the top. If you've been treated rudely by a business employee, who fails to cease being rude, tell the manager or write a letter to the company.

3

"Delighted to Meet You"

Terms of Endearment

QUESTION: I'm a divorced woman with grown children. How should I introduce my "significant other" of three years? I certainly can't use the term boyfriend.

ANSWER: Simply introduce him by using his name. Defining a relationship in an introduction can be a distraction anyway; focus instead on a warm and gracious exchange of names. If you decide to explain your personal relationship, it's more natural to do it in conversation.

In any case, finding a word to define an unmarried relationship can be tricky. Whether your relationship is with someone of the opposite sex or the same sex, terms like partner, live-in, roommate, and my good friend can be confusing and easily misinterpreted. Boyfriend, girlfriend, and special friend seem childishly inappropriate for couples in their thirties and older. And significant other and domestic partner can sound stilted and legalistic. People who get to know you better will soon figure out that you two are romantically involved; details of your personal relationship are probably not that important to others.

FIVE INTRODUCTION GOOFS

Some introduction mistakes are the result of memory lapses or nervousness, but others are entirely preventable. Avoid these foul-ups for smoother introductions:

Looking away. People who look elsewhere while being introduced to someone may be suffering from a case of nerves or self-consciousness, but what their actions say is that they aren't very interested.

Making overly personal comments. Such subjects as divorces, bereavements, job losses, and illnesses make people uncomfortable and should not be raised in introductions.

Interrupting. When someone is engaged in serious conversation or obviously occupied, don't break in to introduce someone else. Wait for a more convenient moment.

Leaving someone out of the post-introduction conversation. Once you've been introduced, don't launch into an animated conversation with the person you've met, leaving the person who's introduced you hanging. Be sure that both parties are included in any conversation that follows an introduction.

Gushing. Most people are embarrassed by overly flattering introductions. Matchmakers take note: Even if you think that two eligible people would be the perfect couple, a low-key introduction is your best bet. Exaggerated praise is likely to be a turnoff.

Name Amnesia

QUESTION: What do I do when I'm introducing someone and suddenly forget their name?

ANSWER: Don't panic. At one time or other, we've all had that awkward moment when we've begun to introduce two acquaintances and then drawn a blank. Just be straightforward: "I'm so embarrassed—I've forgotten your name." Fessing up is far better than ignoring the expected introduction (and person). Sometimes you might even have a chance to instead discreetly ask someone else to tell you the person's name before it's time to make the introduction. If you're the one who's being introduced and suspect someone has forgotten your name, help them out of their jam by extending your hand and saying, "Hello, I'm Susie Smith. It's so nice to meet you." The person who is introducing you will appreciate your thoughtfulness and quick thinking.

THE RIGHT WAY TO MEET AND GREET

It's true: First impressions do count. The image you project when meeting someone for the first time is, in many cases, the picture of you they will always carry with them. If you smile and stay relaxed, make eye contact, shake hands firmly, and greet the person warmly and sincerely, you're likely to make a positive and long-lasting first impression.

Stand up. Today this rule applies to men and women alike. If there's no room to stand—for instance, you're at a restaurant wedged behind a table—briefly lift yourself out of your chair, extend your hand, and say, "Please excuse me for not standing. I'm glad to meet you."

Smile and make eye contact. Your smile conveys warmth and openness; looking a person in the eye clearly shows that you're focused on him or her.

State your greeting. The direct "How do you do?" and "Hello" and "It's so nice to meet you" are all good openers. Repeating the person's name—"I'm pleased to meet you, Ms. Dowd"—not only is polite, but helps you remember the person's name.

Shake hands. Grasp the other person's hand firmly but not too tightly. A proper handshake lasts about three seconds. The clasped hands are pumped two or three times, after which you let go and step back. If you think it sounds silly to mention a specific number of pumps, do remember the last time someone hung on to your hand for a seemingly endless time and you wondered if they would ever let go.

✤

4

Manners at Work

Sneeze in Hand

QUESTION: I noticed a client sneezing into his hand. A few minutes later, my boss introduced me to him. I didn't want to shake his hand, but I did. Was there any other option?

ANSWER: No, not really. You did the right thing (assuming that your next stop was the restroom for a thorough hand washing with soap and hot water). If you didn't shake, the client would have wondered what was wrong with you, and your boss could have been embarrassed or annoyed by your actions. In a social situation, you have a little more leeway—you can claim to be fighting a cold yourself, a perfectly legitimate reason for forgoing a handshake, as long as you offer an apology and an explanation.

BODY LANGUAGE IN OTHER COUNTRIES

When you travel abroad, interpreting body language is important—and challenging. Once you've been in a country for a while, you'll probably get the feel of the local body language. Meanwhile, here are a few guidelines:

- *Personal space.* The distance maintained between yourself and others is important; getting too close or moving too far away can be misconstrued as unwanted familiarity or standoffishness. North Americans and Europeans are comfortable standing some two to three feet apart. The Japanese and other Asians require more space, but most of the rest of the world likes to get closer.

- *Handshakes.* In North America and Europe, a firm handshake is an appropriate form of greeting. In Asia and the Middle East, where hand shaking is still relatively new, the customary grip is gentler; a too-hearty grip could be interpreted as aggressive. In Islamic countries, offering your hand to a woman is highly offensive. At the other extreme, it's said that you can never shake hands too much in France, where women shake hands as freely and as often as men.

- *Bowing and similar greetings.* In Japan and some other Asian countries, the bow is the equivalent of the handshake. In rank-conscious Japan, the person of inferior rank bows first and lowest. The Indians and Thai may place their hands together at the chest in a prayerlike gesture as a form of greeting.

- *Touching.* North Americans don't engage in casual touching, but Latin Americans and southern Europeans often do. If a native jabs you with his finger to make a point or touches your arm in conversation, don't be offended. In the Middle East, and in Southeast Asian and Pacific Island nations, a man may even find his male host taking his hand. Do not misconstrue these gestures, but don't try to copy them, either.

�֍

Smelly Situations

QUESTION: My coworker has really bad body odor. Colleagues joke about it behind his back. I feel bad for him and would like to help. Should I broach the subject?

ANSWER: Surveys show that most people would want to be told, preferably by a friend, if they had an offensive body odor. If you two aren't really good friends, however, don't bring it up. It's not worth the risk of humiliating or angering him. His problem might be caused by a medical condition. If you are close friends or if he has a good friend in the office, either you or his friend could say, "I need to discuss something with you that's difficult for me to bring up, but that I'd want you to tell me if the shoe was on the other foot. I also want you to know that I care about you and want you to succeed here. That's why I'm telling you, as a friend, that your body odor is an issue." You may be able to recommend something that has worked for you. Tell him that the discussion about his problem will stay private, and be sure it does. If there is no one at the office who feels close enough to talk to him about the problem, you could mention it, confidentially, to someone in human resources, who can talk with him.

CUBICLE COURTESY

Those who work cheek-by-jowl with others need to be extra considerate, since every sound and smell they emit affects everyone nearby. Here are the top manners minefields for cubicle-dwellers and how to avoid them:

What is that smell? Bringing food into the workplace? Spicy or smelly foods like greasy subs, cooked broccoli, and garlic bread should not be eaten at your desk. Try the lunchroom, kitchen, lounge, an empty conference room, or outdoors. Also, go easy on the perfume or cologne and do what you can to prevent body odor.

Big primping. Applying nail polish, massaging your feet, cutting your nails (nail clipper alert!), combing your hair, or putting on makeup is not appropriate at your desk. Save it for the bathroom or, better yet, do it at home.

Noise pollution. Be conscious of your contribution to office noise and how distracting it is to others. Keep your voice modulated when talking on the phone, limit personal phone calls, and don't use the speakerphone or play music others can hear. Likewise, keep conversations with coworkers sotto voce or step into a conference room or hallway.

No privacy. Just because their door is always open doesn't mean cubicle workers are always available. You can't effectively knock, but you can, and should, ask if you can come in. And keep "prairie-dogging"—standing up or hanging over the wall to speak to the person in the neighboring cubicle—to a minimum. If the coworker you want to speak with is on the phone, don't hover. Try again later.

✱

Damage Control for
Email Bloopers

QUESTION: I just trashed my boss in an email and then sent it to her instead of my friend in accounting! What should I do?

ANSWER: Own up to your mistake immediately. Seek out your boss before she comes to you and say, "I can't believe I did such a stupid thing. I'm so sorry." If the comments you made in the email expressed frustration with the way your boss is handling things, use this as a chance to discuss the problem. If it was a personal attack, just apologize profusely and do your best to see that the damage is mended over time.

THE GOLDEN RULES OF
EMAIL ETIQUETTE

1. **IF YOU CAN'T POST IT ON A BULLETIN BOARD FOR EVERYONE TO READ, DON'T SEND IT.** Stories abound about the "private" email that became a public embarrassment. Nothing is private on email; it's all too easy for sensitive information to end up in the wrong in-box.

2. **HIT SEND ONLY WHEN YOU'RE SURE YOUR MESSAGE IS READY TO GO.** Let it simmer for a little while, rereading your

cyber-communication before sending. Hold any messages that may be delicate, using the Draft or Send Later feature as a safety net.

3. **NIX THE TEMPTATION TO HIDE BEHIND EMAIL.** Discuss the most sensitive topics in person or on the phone. You're about to fire an employee via email? Forget about it, and do the deed person to person.

4. **MAKE IT EASY TO READ.** Use a simple, clear font. Avoid using all capitals in your emails. They're the email equivalent of yelling and are also difficult to read.

5. **CHECK YOUR SPELLING AND GRAMMAR.** Even a simple emailed message begs for some standards, especially when you're sending professional correspondence.

6. **ANNOUNCE YOUR MESSAGE.** Use of the subject line helps the recipient sort the mail in order of priority.

7. **FORGO THE JOKES AND CHAIN LETTERS.** Send the personal spam only if you know it's welcome.

8. **RESPECT PRIVACY.** Don't share others' email addresses unless you know they don't mind.

✳

The Importance of
Being Punctual

QUESTION: I was five minutes late for a job interview because it took me longer than I expected to get there. I didn't get the job, even though I was more than qualified. Was my lateness the reason?

ANSWER: Most likely your tardiness did you in. There is one inviolable rule for job interviews: Be on time. First impressions are lasting, and if you keep your interviewer waiting, it will be very difficult to recover from the poor impression you've made. Prevent it from happening next time: Do a trial run by traveling to the company a day or two before the interview to learn how long it takes to get there—and then factor in some extra time (ten to twenty minutes) to ensure that you're on time on the day of your interview. If you really are unavoidably late, it's imperative that you call to alert those you're inconveniencing. Apologize profusely (no made-up stories), give an estimate of when you'll arrive, and ask if they would prefer to reschedule. Note that if something truly beyond your control has been the cause of your delay (a train breakdown, a sudden ice storm), you'll probably receive a more sympathetic reception.

DEAL MAKERS, NOT BREAKERS

There is so much advice thrown at those interviewing for jobs that the most important points can get lost. Here are the five things that will give you a clear edge in a job interview:

1. **BE PUNCTUAL.** Plan to arrive early to ensure that you are calm, collected, and on time—no matter what. Allow an extra ten to twenty minutes for your travel time; and if you are really thirty minutes early, wait elsewhere until five (or even ten) minutes before your scheduled interview.

2. **BE PREPARED.** Read up on the company or organization through industry trade magazines and Web sites. Have a sense of the company's products, markets, and plans for growth. Prepare to talk about your aptitude and experience and, especially, your strengths. Review your resume, refreshing your memory with dates of employment and job titles. If necessary, revise the resume to highlight areas of experience most relevant to the job you're applying for. Ask your spouse, a family member, or a friend to role-play the interview with you, or practice alone, asking yourself the questions you're likely to be asked and then answering them aloud.

3. **DRESS FOR SUCCESS.** It's a fact of interview life that appearance matters. To get your wardrobe right, briefly stop by the company's reception area in the days or weeks before the interview and note how people dress. If you can't make a pre-interview visit, call and ask a human resources representative or someone you know there about the dress code. When selecting interview clothes, go one better than the company's standard office wear. For example, if the men normally wear slacks and a sport shirt, wear slacks with a shirt and tie and a blazer or sport coat. Don't overdo it by wearing anything flashy or attention-getting, like a loud, bright-colored shirt

or gaudy jewelry. And turn a critical eye to your coat, umbrella, and pocketbook and/or briefcase—they're part of your interview wardrobe and should be presentable, too.

4. **BE ENGAGING.** Smile, be energetic, and look your interviewer in the eye. This is your chance to demonstrate that you'll represent the company well and that you are a confident, can-do person. Being sincerely enthusiastic and friendly goes a long way toward having a positive interview—and leaving a favorable impression.

5. **SAY "THANK YOU"—TWICE.** The first thank-you comes at the end of the interview, along with eye contact and a firm handshake. It should be a clear statement—"I really appreciate your taking the time to talk to me about the position"—not a mumbled "thanks." That night or the next day, write your second thank-you. Your note can either be handwritten (legibly) or word-processed—and in some cases it can be emailed. It's up to you to decide the most appropriate way to send it. Pen and paper (snail mail) is more traditional and the best choice in most cases. You may decide to email your thank-you, however, to a dot-com or a tech company. An emailed thank-you is also faster if the interviewer is traveling or making a decision about final interviews within the next day or two after your interview. You can always follow up your email with a written note. Your note doesn't need to be lengthy, but it should recap your strong points and answer any questions that may have arisen during the interview. End the letter by thanking the interviewer and expressing your hope for a positive outcome. Put your note aside to reread once more before mailing, to be sure it's error-free.

❊

Gifting Up

QUESTION: My boss always gives me a gift at the holidays. Should I give him one, too?

ANSWER: Generally, no. It could be perceived as trying to curry favor. However, a joint gift from you and other employees that isn't too expensive or personal is fine. Or, if you and your boss have worked closely together for years, it's okay to give a small present.

WHO GETS A GIFT AT WORK?

Should I Give Holiday Gifts to the People Who Report to Me?

You're the boss, so it's your choice! It's certainly a nice gesture and a great way to acknowledge your staff. If you give gifts, do so across the board—don't give to only one department head, leaving out the other two. Good gift ideas include tasty gourmet food items; gift certificates; tickets to the theater or a sporting event; books, CDs, or DVDs; and nice bottles of wine.

What About Coworkers?

The "Secret Santa" system (in which each employee draws a name and gives a gift to that person) and the holiday grab bag are two easy, fun ways to handle gift giving with coworkers. (Or try a "Yankee Swap," where numbers are drawn and anonymous gifts are opened and traded.) These gift exchanges keep costs down and can be a lot of fun. Humorous gifts are okay if they don't go too far (no tasteless, off-color items). Edible gifts are easy and economical: You can bring in a batch of cookies or a box of chocolates to share with your colleagues.

And Clients?

Company policy typically dictates whether you can give and receive gifts from clients and vendors. If gifts are allowed, usually there are cost limits (typically $25). If you plan to give a gift to a client, check his company's policy first. Token gifts from business associates are generally fine, especially during the holidays. If you receive a gift that violates company policy, it's important to return it—with a gracious explanation so as not to embarrass the giver.

The Limits of Generosity

QUESTION: How do I politely turn down requests from coworkers to donate to a charity or purchase items for a fund-raiser?

ANSWER: Don't refuse all requests, since you'll come across as less than generous. But repeated requests from coworkers to open your wallet for various causes can make you feel like you're being nickel-and-dimed to death. If you don't want to contribute, simply say, "I wish I could, but I'm afraid I can't give this time." If you've just contributed to another organization, explain that you can give only so much each year and that you hope the person understands. Some offices have guidelines that limit collections; if yours doesn't, you could suggest instituting one.

THE RIGHT WORDS WHEN . . .

A coworker becomes engaged or married. You could say, "Best wishes! I wish you much happiness!" Or, "I'm so happy for you! What are your plans?" Genuinely wish your coworker well. Don't be overly inquisitive about the choice of spouse (that's what in-laws are for!), and don't be too free with marriage advice or horror stories.

A coworker is pregnant. Express your happiness, but don't pry into personal details. Refrain from giving advice unless it's asked for, and avoid giving any that may conflict with current medical opinion. And it's in poor taste to share details of your own labor and childbirth, or any horror stories that you've heard.

A coworker miscarries. A miscarriage is a death that requires grieving. Be sympathetic by recognizing the depth of the loss and by being there for your friend if she wants to talk about it. Never say, "It was for the best," or, "It was God's will." And never, under any circumstances, imply that the miscarriage may have resulted from something your coworker did or did not do.

A coworker divorces. Divorce is another kind of death. It's better to listen than to talk, although you might offer practical advice, such as how to find child care or file income taxes, if asked. And whatever you do, don't say awful things about your coworker's soon-to-be former spouse ("I've wondered when you'd get rid of that louse!"). A simple response—no matter the circumstances—is "I'm sorry. Thanks for telling me."

A coworker is ill. When a coworker or a coworker's relative is seriously ill, actions speak louder than words. Show sympathy by helping the person at work and not complaining about absences. Be alert if anyone tries to undermine the worker's position during the illness or to loot his office or files (it happens). Keep the person in the loop, if he's receptive, about what's happening in the office.

A coworker loses a loved one. Write, and speak, your condolences. If you're close, attend pre-funeral and funeral services. If you aren't close, don't use the occasion as an excuse to take a day off. Never make comments such as "It was a blessing" and "Be thankful his suffering is over." The death of a loved one will deeply affect your coworker, so don't expect him or her to bounce back in a few weeks' time.

A coworker is fired or the victim of downsizing. Be sympathetic, but don't prolong the agony by talking it into the ground. Accept your coworker's official explanation for the firing, and don't engage in speculation with him or anyone else about the cause. If you can give practical assistance, do so—a recommendation, help with a resume update, job leads.

5

Getting the Word Out

Signing Off on Holiday Cards

QUESTION: Is it tacky to send holiday cards with your name printed inside? It's so much easier than signing 100 cards.

ANSWER: Holiday cards printed with your name in lieu of a signature are more appropriate for business use, but sometimes people use this shortcut for their personal holiday cards because they're so pressed for time. The manners police won't ticket you for using printed holiday cards, but it's warmer and more personal to sign each card to your friends yourself. Some ideas for taking the pressure off: Shorten your list, start earlier, or choose a different, less hectic holiday such as New Year's to send your greetings.

NOTEWORTHY NEWSLETTERS

Another holiday greetings shortcut is to send newsletters, which are basically form letters recapping a family's personal news for the year. At their best, these letters are an efficient and fun way to update friends and relatives on family news; at their worst, they're impersonal turnoffs that earn their nickname, "Brag and Gag" letters. Here are some suggestions on how to create a holiday newsletter that will be an enjoyable read—not an annoyance or the butt of holiday jokes.

Do

- Send holiday newsletters only to those you think will really be interested in family news.
- Keep your letter to one page or less.
- Keep it positive and not too personal.
- Include a handwritten personal salutation—"Dear Kathy and Dale"—rather than the stilted "Dear Friends."
- Sign each letter individually to personalize it more. If you can, include a short friendly note, like "How is your new house? We would love to hear from you!"

Don't

- Brag. "Sam and I were lucky enough to visit Europe last September" is fine, but "Sam and I spent a week at one of France's top resorts and were utterly pampered" screams "Eat your heart out!" So does reporting on your teenager's near-perfect SAT scores.
- Include boring or gruesome details. People don't want to read a blow-by-blow account of little Tim's T-ball season or your recent bunion surgery.

�֍

Group Dinner Dilemma

QUESTION: How do I invite others to a restaurant but let them know that they'll have to pay for their own meals?

ANSWER: It's all in how you phrase it. Call your friends or relatives and say, "John, would you and Ellen like to meet us at Jackson's Place on Saturday night? We're asking Michelle and Eric, too. We thought it would be fun for the six of us to have a night out together. Just let me know if you can come and I'll make the reservation." By posing your request this way, it's clear that you're just the social coordinator and not the host, so everyone should understand that they're paying for their own meal. However, if you said, "We're hosting a dinner at Jackson's Place," or sent a written invitation with that wording, your guests would be right to assume that dinner is on you.

THE RIGHT INVITE

Invitations should include the basics of who, what, when, where, and why. Sometimes there's other information your guests would appreciate knowing, too. Here's how to keep them in the loop:

Dress code. On formal invitations, notations such as "Black tie" and "White tie" are printed or written in the lower right corner. On informal invitations, it's not necessary to mention a dress code, but guests will welcome any guidance you can give, such as "Casual dress," "Business casual," "No jeans, please," or "Jackets required." If there's nothing on the invitation about dress, and the recipient is left wondering, it's okay to ask the host or others who are invited.

"No gifts, please." Once considered a no-no (and still inappropriate on wedding invitations), it's now okay to include the notation "No gifts, please" at the bottom of an invitation, such as one to an anniversary party. Or you can tell invitees in person or by phone.

"Bring your bathing suit." If you'd like your guests to bring anything special, say so on the invitation. "The pool is open! Don't forget your suit and towel."

Potluck. These suppers, in which all guests contribute food, are a fun and easy way for family and friends to share their favorite dishes and an evening together. It's important to be clear that it's a potluck, so write it on the invitation or tell people if you're inviting them in person. You might also want to assign food categories (appetizer, salad, casserole) to keep the menu varied. This can also be noted on the invitation.

BYOB/BYOF. BYOB on an invitation means "Bring your own bottle"; guests bring their beverages and the hosts supply glasses, ice, and possibly mixers and/or appetizers. BYOF means "Bring your own food." Guests come with food for themselves, not dishes to be shared (though they may if they wish). Technically, these events are "organized," not "hosted." An important note: BYOB invitations mean that the guests should plan on leaving any unused alcoholic beverages with the hosts. In most states in the U.S., it's illegal to drive with opened containers or bottles of alcoholic beverages. On the other hand, after BYOF or potluck parties, it's customary for guests to ask the hosts if they would like to keep any leftover food or if they would rather that guests take the leftovers home. Either way is okay.

When will the party be over? Generally, it isn't considered polite or necessary to include ending times on invitations, but there are exceptions. They include invitations to children's parties (parents need to know when to return for their kids) and invitations to parties that precede other events, such as a cocktail party before a play and a brunch before a business meeting. In these cases, an end time is included to allow guests to get to the next location. End times are also included for open houses, when guests are free to come and go during the specified hours.

How to Unfriend on Facebook – Especially When It's Your Ex-Boyfriend

QUESTION: My boyfriend and I just broke up. We are friends on Facebook, and also share many mutual friends. Should we unfriend each other?

ANSWER: It's OK to unfriend your former boyfriend. One part of moving on when a relationship ends is severing the ties. If your ex unfriends you, understand it's part of the process of breaking up. There's also nothing inherently wrong for people who have an amicable break-up to remain Facebook friends. Just make sure your relationship reflects that you aren't together any longer, and keep any messages or posts to one another on a strictly platonic "friend" level to avoid sending the wrong message to your ex, your other friends, or anyone new you might be dating.

COMMON RULES OF THE ROAD:
FACEBOOK AND OTHER SOCIAL NETWORKING SITES

Regardless of which social networking sites you use, each has its own rules. Be sure to check those rules and then be prepared to abide by them if you want to remain a member.

• Posting. Avoid posting "too much information." This could mean too many banal updates, such as what you ate for breakfast, or it could mean updates that are too personal in nature, such as relationship or medical details. Also, strive to avoid negative posts.

• Photographs. Choose the images you post of yourself thoughtfully, and be especially careful when posting images of other people on your page. Don't post anything that would be embarrassing to the people in the photos. It's always best to ask someone before posting their photo. The easiest time to do is when you first take the picture: "Would it be all right if I post this on Facebook?"

• Tags. You can and should untag yourself from any photos with which you are uncomfortable. Remember: this won't remove the image from the Internet; it only removes links that identify you. If you really feel embarrassed or upset by the image, ask the person who posted it to take it down immediately.

• Privacy Settings. Learn how to use privacy settings to limit the content others can share on your site. Just don't count on them to be a final protection: If you really don't want some people to see what you post, it's best not to post it at all.

• Friending. You don't have to accept everyone who requests to be friends with you, especially strangers.

• Unfriending. It's okay to unfriend someone if you are no longer comfortable remaining connected to them, but don't unfriend and refriend over minor tiffs. If you do choose to go the route of unfriending, think about your offline relationship with that person to determine whether or not you want to explain why you plan to stop being friends on Facebook.

✣

6

The Perfectly Polite Date

Breakup Basics

QUESTION: I'm ready to end a relationship. Is it better to break the news in a public place, such as a café, or in my home?

ANSWER: Meet privately. It's better to give the person you're breaking up with the courtesy of not being observed by other people during such a traumatic time. It's therefore inappropriate to stage a breakup in public in hopes that the presence of others will keep things calm; delivering your news in a quiet place like your home—or even at a remote table at a restaurant—would be the kinder way to go. Think of the other person's feelings. Be sure that he's reasonably in control before leaving. Someone who's extremely upset or angry should not be driving or going off on their own. Just because you're ending the relationship doesn't mean it's okay to ignore concerns for your ex's safety and well-being.

GETTING BACK TO DATING

For someone who has lost a spouse through divorce or death or experienced the breakup of a long-standing relationship, it can be very difficult to begin dating again, and people often put their social lives on hold. But sooner or later, most people decide it's time to take the plunge and reenter the dating pool. When that time comes, it can be helpful to consider the following do's and don'ts:

Do give yourself permission to enjoy yourself and the companionship of other adults. Dating is not a lifelong commitment. It's an opportunity to get to know someone else, do something different, and have fun for a few hours.

Do understand that times have changed. If you're nervous about the new dating rituals, talk with some of your contemporaries who date to get a clearer picture of how things are done in your social group. Dating customs can vary considerably among regional, cultural, and age groups, and you'll feel more confident when you know what to expect.

Do set fundamental standards for yourself and your dates. Decide what you hope to gain from dating—friendship or something more. Think about the qualities you look for in potential companions or partners and evaluate your own assets. You'll probably discover that your expectations of others have changed radically since your earlier dating days, and that you have a lot more to offer than you were aware of.

Do tell dates about your family responsibilities. If you have children (whether you're the custodial or noncustodial parent) or if you're the caregiver for a family member, it's only fair to tell anyone you date about your responsibilities. Besides, it's better to know at the outset whether someone is or isn't interested in a relationship that comes complete with a family.

Do let your children know you're dating and introduce them to your dates. Be aware that children of any age naturally have questions, which stem from concern for their parent or worries about how a new relationship could affect the family. Children not only need reassurance, but also need to understand that their parent has a right to a social life.

Don't be embarrassed to express your feelings and preferences and to ask questions of a date. If you're more comfortable sharing expenses, say so. Be willing to offer suggestions and alternatives when someone asks what you'd like to do or suggests an activity that you'd rather not do.

Shy About Meeting On-Line

QUESTION: I met my boyfriend one year ago through an on-line dating service. We're often asked, "How did you two meet?" I'm uncomfortable talking about it. What's a noncommittal but honest answer to the question?

ANSWER: There's no shame in admitting that you met your boyfriend on-line through a dating service. People meet on-line every day, and it can be a great way to connect. However, if you're uncomfortable about it, you don't need to share your "how we met" story. Instead, reply with an entertaining story about one of your first dates: "Well, a better story is what happened on our third date, when Stan took me skiing for the first time." You could also say you met on a blind date (which is true). If the person presses for more information, change the subject. Say, "Let's not talk about that; it's old news. Want to hear about the cruise we're taking in January?"

INTERNET DATING ETIQUETTE

Despite any promised safeguards, on-line dating services are relatively new, and security measures and client etiquette can still be considered "under construction." The following tips should help subscribers get the most for their investment of time and money:

- Use a reputable service. Check it out before you sign on. How? Get referrals from friends or search for message boards where people discuss their experiences.
- Be honest when writing your profile, and post only an up-to-date photo. Proofread the profile carefully.
- Respond when someone contacts you, even when you aren't interested—a quick message expressing thanks and a courteous regret will do. If you're no longer available, say so, but don't use this excuse if you continue to use the service and your cybername.
- If someone uses inappropriate or offensive language, don't reply. If the approaches continue, notify the service.
- Protect yourself by not giving out any personal information—last name, home address, phone number, email address, or office address and number.
- Arrange first meetings in a public place and limit the duration. An hour should be long enough to decide if you want to meet again. Tell a friend or family member where you'll be and how long you expect the meeting to last.

Some services are better than others at screening out undesirable contacts, and a smart user will take other people's profiles with a grain of salt. It's human to exaggerate one's good points, and especially easy on the Internet. If you're interested in a person but not quite sure about his claims, trust your instincts and curtail any contact that seems odd or makes you uncomfortable.

✳

To Pay or Not to Pay? Dating Dilemmas

QUESTION: I'm newly single and just met a guy that I'd like to go out with. Is it okay for me to ask him out? If I ask, does that mean I should pay?

ANSWER: Surveys show that most men still like to be the one to ask a woman out, and most women still prefer being asked. But like so many customs today, the issue of who asks is not carved in stone. If you want to go out with him and he hasn't asked, don't stand on ceremony—go ahead and pop the question. It could be the start of a beautiful relationship! By inviting him out, you are in effect saying that you intend to pay. Unless both of you agree in advance to overturn the tradition of the host paying or you've decided to share expenses, the person who asks should foot the bill. However, if you're at the theater or restaurant and your date insists on paying for his half, don't get into a skirmish over the bill. Thank him and accept his offer graciously.

EQUAL-OPPORTUNITY CHIVALRY

Thankfully, chivalry is not dead. But today, it's not so much about men rescuing and protecting women as it is about being considerate of others. Holding the door for the person behind you, helping a friend put on his coat, standing to greet a newcomer—a polite person should extend these gestures to everyone, regardless of gender. Of course, if a man insists on playing the perfect gentleman, and is especially attentive to a woman, she shouldn't be offended. Whatever his motive, he's still trying to be kind.

Here are some long-standing chivalries, updated and made gender-neutral:

- **Holding the door.** Whoever gets to the door first holds it for others.
- **Getting off an elevator.** The person closest to the door exits first.
- **Helping to put on a coat.** Anyone having trouble putting on a coat or sweater should receive some help, regardless of gender.
- **Paying for a meal.** Whoever does the inviting does the paying.
- **Standing.** Getting up to greet someone is always polite—and this is especially important when the person is elderly or is a business superior or client. It's also the thing to do when you're being introduced to someone.
- **Walking on the outside.** The custom of a man walking between his female companion and the street was the custom in the days when carriages splashed mud and ladies' finery needed shielding. These days, it doesn't matter who is walking on the street side of the sidewalk.
- **Shaking hands.** Used to be that a man was supposed to wait for a woman to offer her hand before he extended his. Today, regardless of gender, people should shake hands upon meeting, and it doesn't matter who puts out their hand first.
- **Helping to carry something.** A neighbor or coworker—anyone—who is overloaded with books or packages will appreciate an offer of help from whoever is nearby.

❈

7

Family Matters

Pass the Turkey, Hold the Dirty Jokes; or, Keeping Dinner Conversations Clean

QUESTION: Is there a way to keep my husband's grandfather from telling inappropriate jokes and stories at the Thanksgiving dinner table? We love having him over, but my eight-year-old son is getting quite an education!

ANSWER: Establish some "house rules" and then share them with your husband's grandfather weeks before the gathering. Say, "Pop, we can't wait to see you on the 26th, but we have to ask you to save the off-color jokes for after dinner—and away from the children." Let him know that his stories offend some family members and aren't appropriate for young listeners. Ask him to refrain so the meal is pleasant for the whole group. Don't lecture him or tell him he has to change; just stress that in your house, holidays are G-rated. Nothing is fool-proof, though, so unless you're willing to dis-invite him (a hurtful step I wouldn't recommend)—be prepared to change the subject quickly should his conversation range into R-rated territory.

A FAMILY GATHERING SURVIVAL GUIDE

Extended families often get together for holidays, birthdays, and family reunions—and some who live close to one another gather more regularly. Cut down on the stress and focus on the fun with these survival tips:

Spread the responsibilities around. Offer to help when a family member holds a get-together. If you live close by, alternate locations for events. At the party, adults should take turns watching the kids.

Adapt to different entertaining styles. Your sister-in-law likes to prepare everything herself, you prefer a potluck, and Uncle Jim insists on taking everyone out to eat. Celebrate the variety.

Don't bring family problems to the party. This is not the time to complain. Negative talk about someone who isn't present will probably get back to them and cause hurt feelings. Refrain from picking on those you're visiting with, as well.

Indulge the family storytellers. As long as the tales aren't at the expense of someone else, stories from the past (even if oft-repeated) are how younger generations and new in-laws learn the family's history.

Accept one another's quirks. Be tolerant of harmless idiosyncrasies.

�֍

Holiday Visiting Marathon

QUESTION: My husband and I married last July, and both our parents have invited us for the holidays. We'd love to see everyone, but we all live hundreds of miles apart. To visit with both families would mean spending most of our holiday on the road or in airports.

ANSWER: With so many families separated by distance these days, this is a common dilemma. You and your husband have to decide what you want to do. You might take turns visiting one family this Christmas and the other next year. Flip a coin to avoid any appearance of favoritism. (Some couples who alternate the years with their families also include Thanksgiving in the mix: This year, it's Christmas with his family, Thanksgiving with hers. Next year, it's the reverse. This way, you see both families at holiday times each year.) Another option is to host both sets of parents at Christmas—though a large gathering of out-of-town guests presents its own set of stresses. Or you might spend your first Christmas on your own and visit with your families at a less busy time. It's unlikely that either set of parents wants your holiday to be an endurance test, so if you take the time to explain your situation and feelings, they should be understanding. If you decide not to travel, call your parents on Christmas at a time when you'll have a chance to chat at length.

STAYING WITH RELATIVES

Follow these etiquette essentials when you stay with relatives. Treat host family members with the same respect and consideration you would friends.

Establish convenient dates for visits. Invitations to visit family are usually casual, but it's still important to consider your relatives' schedules and responsibilities. Consult about plans well in advance.

Avoid surprises. Don't drop in for the weekend unexpectedly. Leave pets at home or in a boarding facility unless your hosts insist that your animal come along.

Consider the hosting family's capabilities. If Aunt Maggie recently sold her five-bedroom house and moved to a small condo, it's unlikely she can accommodate you, your spouse, and children. Staying at a nearby hotel or B&B would be considerate, as well as perhaps the only feasible way to go.

Set specific arrival and departure dates and times. Avoid vague itineraries like, "We'll be there Thursday or Friday, Saturday at the latest." If you can't pin down an arrival time, stay overnight at a motel rather than arriving on a family member's doorstep at three in the morning.

Be gracious. A thank-you note and gift for your relative hosts is always appreciated. If you visit frequently, notes and gifts aren't required every time, though saying "thank you" is.

Help out and clean up. Volunteer your help and pitch in with daily chores. Be neat.

Prepare your children for the visit, too. Brief your kids on what you expect of them when they're visiting their relatives. Set a good example; when they see you picking up your belongings and helping in the kitchen, they'll be more likely to do the same— even if you need to remind them. Reinforce the ideas of respecting others' property and privacy.

Leave on time. If you must delay your departure, be sure it's okay with your host. Move to other lodgings if an extended stay is likely to cause stress.

Too Much of a Good Thing

QUESTION: Last Christmas, both sets of grandparents gave our five-year-old son an avalanche of gifts. This year, my husband and I would like to downplay the material side of the holidays. How can we persuade our parents to scale back?

ANSWER: Begin by trying to see it from their perspective. For grandparents, the great joy of gift giving is watching their grandchild's eyes light up with joy at the sight of a present. They may also enjoy the opportunity to be more generous than they could be when their own children were young. With that in mind, you and your husband might tell each set of grandparents that you'd like to simplify the holidays and encourage your son to focus not just on toys but on the important people in his life (including his grandparents). Say that you're giving him fewer things, and that you hope they'll cut back as well. However, be prepared for them to ignore your request. They may feel that while you're entitled to your approach, so are they. To downplay materialism in a different way, ask them to give your son the gift of their time (making cookies with him, building a snowman, going to a local Christmas concert) along with their other gifts.

WHAT'S IN A (GRANDPARENT'S) NAME?

Grandpa, Gramps, Grammy, Grandma—there are endless versions of grandparent nicknames. The only "rule" is that the name the grandparent is called be one that he or she can live with, for a long time!

Once their first child is born, new parents often begin to address their own parents the same way they addressed their grandparents—as "Nana" and "Gramps," for example. Sometimes a new nickname evolves when a toddler grandchild christens his grandparent with one of his own words: Enter "Boppa" or "Mimi" or something equally unique.

If everyone is happy with a grandparent nickname, by all means stick with it. But grandparents who aren't shouldn't hesitate to make their preference clear. Explain to the new parents that you are uncomfortable with your assigned name or title. Let the family know what name you prefer and ask for their help in establishing that name with your grandchild or step-grandchild.

When choosing a name or title, give consideration to the long-term consequences. The name will probably work its way through the entire family, so if you're not happy with it, speak up before it becomes permanent.

�֍

Torn Between Divorced Parents

QUESTION: My parents are divorced and not on good terms. It's uncomfortable if they're both at social events, but I don't want to exclude them from family get-togethers such as holidays and my children's birthdays. When they both invite us to their houses for the same holiday, how do we manage to keep from running ourselves ragged or choosing one and hurting the other's feelings? We also have my husband's parents to consider.

ANSWER: Your sensitivity is admirable, but your priority is with your own family and the creation of your own pleasant holiday traditions. Don't make your parents' hostile relationship your problem. Be frank with each parent, telling them that you want your family's special times to be relaxed and happy for your children. This means you can't spend Christmas driving to one parent's home and then to the other's, and then to your husband's parents'. Consider taking turns celebrating an event on its real date with one parent and then having a second celebration on another day with the other. Don't allow your parents to put you in the middle. Remind them that you love them both, but insist that your children be able to spend time with all their grandparents in a harmonious atmosphere. Assuming that both your parents are otherwise lovely people, ask your in-laws if your mother or father could be invited to a holiday celebration at their house. For those once-in-a-lifetime events that can't be duplicated (like christenings, graduations, recitals, and weddings), ask your parents if, for the sake of their grandchildren, they could bury the hatchet for the day so no one misses out.

"WE'RE GETTING DIVORCED": HOW *NOT* TO RESPOND

- "No wonder you seem so stressed!"
- "Was she having an affair?"
- "I hope you take him for every penny."
- "I feel bad for your children. It's going to be tough for them."
- "I guess you'll be selling the house now."
- "I always thought he was a jerk."
- "I'm surprised it lasted this long."

Questions and comments of this sort run the gamut from presumptuous to downright mean. Though there's no all-purpose response to the news, try to say something that shows concern without prying, such as, "Thanks for letting me know. I wish you the best."

How should a divorced or separated person reply to thoughtless comments? With a large grain of salt. Without being rude, you can ignore or defuse the remark or question ("It's all for the best" or "I really don't discuss it") and turn the conversation in another direction.

✵

8

Kid Stuff

First-Name Basis

QUESTION: Where we live the adults encourage kids to call them by their first names, but my husband and I were raised to address adults by "Mr." or "Mrs." Should we let our children go along with the crowd or stick to what feels right for us?

ANSWER: It's fine for children to call adults by their first names, as long as the adults say they prefer it and the children's parents approve. As this casual form of address becomes more common in many communities, it can be hard for parents to go against the grain—but there's nothing wrong with doing so. In fact, it's still most respectful for children to start out addressing adults by titles (Miss, Ms., Mr., Mrs., Dr.) with last names, until an adult requests otherwise. In that case, it's up to the parents whether to let them make the exception; most do let their kids go along with such requests. Regarding your particular situation, if you're truly uncomfortable letting your children make any exceptions requested by adults, you might consider compromises. You could agree that first names are okay for your closest friends. Or, you could have your children use titles ("Mrs." "Dr.," "Mr.") with first names, such as "Miss June" and "Mr. Bill." When speaking with your kids, refer to adults in the same way you want them to ("Mr. and Mrs. Todd are coming over" or "Mrs. Cindy has a dog"). Since using titles isn't the norm where you live, you'll probably have to remind your kids often not to use first names when first introduced to adults.

TEACHING KIDS HOW TO MEET AND GREET

Playacting and practicing will help your children learn to meet and greet both adults and kids with greater ease. Children as young as age five can master these tips:

1. IF YOU'RE SEATED, STAND UP.

2. SMILE!

3. LOOK THE PERSON IN THE EYE.

4. MOVE TOWARD THE PERSON TO OFFER A HANDSHAKE—ESPECIALLY IF IT'S SOMEONE YOU'RE MEETING FOR THE FIRST TIME.

5. SAY THE PERSON'S NAME AS YOU'RE GREETING HIM: "HI, MR. BLOOM, IT'S NICE TO SEE YOU AGAIN."

6. UNLESS IT'S JUST A QUICK "HELLO," BE READY TO RESPOND TO AN ADULT'S GREETING PLEASANTLY WITH SOMETHING LIKE "I'M FINE, THANK YOU!" OR TO ADD A COMMENT OF YOUR OWN, LIKE "HOW ARE YOU?" OR "FUN PARTY, ISN'T IT?"

7. WHEN ANOTHER PERSON SAYS "HI" TO YOU, BE SURE TO RESPOND WITH YOUR OWN "HI."

❋

When Playdates
Become Fightdates

QUESTION: My three-year-old just started having playdates. What do I do if a child hits her or grabs her toy? I don't want to discipline someone else's child, but I don't want my daughter to be bullied.

ANSWER: Three-year-olds are just beginning to learn how to share and play nicely together. Before your daughter has a friend over, talk with the other parent about discipline so you're prepared for problems that may arise. You might say, "This is one of Patricia's first playdates. How would you like me to handle it if one of the children acts up? When Patricia gets too excited, I take her into another room to calm her down for a few minutes." If the kids start to fight over a particular toy, try to distract them with another toy or activity. If a child is physically rough with your child, don't hesitate to intervene. Say, "Jenna! Stop!" and gently lift your child away. Later, calmly tell the other parent what happened, and leave the discipline to her. If the kids get together again and your daughter's little friend is still too rough, you may want to put a hold on future playdates until the child is a bit older (and, hopefully, calmer!).

PLAYDATE ETIQUETTE

Playdates offer great socializing opportunities for children and, most important, can be lots of fun. They can be convenient, too: Once the children feel comfortable in each other's homes, one parent can watch the children while the other gets a much-needed hour or two of free time. Establish the rules with other parents in advance.

Set clear starting and ending times and stick to them. Always be on time to pick up your child. If you must arrive early, return late, or cancel the playdate, let the other parent know as soon as you can.

Be clear about whether the other parent should stay. When you first get your toddlers together, it's a good idea for both parents to stay with the children. This allows the visiting child to get used to new people and surroundings. As the relationship grows, toddlers can be left with one parent and for longer periods. If you live some distance apart, it may be more convenient for the other parent to stay for the playdate, so be prepared to welcome her for the duration of the visit. Discuss these arrangements ahead of time.

Consult about feeding, health, and other care issues. What kinds of snacks are acceptable? Is your little guest allergic to anything? If you have a pet, tell the other parent. Children may be allergic to, or fearful of, animals, so you may have to keep Fluffy outside or in the crate. If your child is on medication or has special health needs, don't expect the other parent to be a nurse. Never leave your child with anyone who isn't qualified for and agreeable to the responsibility. If your child is ill—with or without a fever—cancel the playdate as soon as possible.

Provide all the necessary supplies when your child is the guest. This can include diapers, wipes, hats, mittens, and boots.

Have plenty of toys and activities on hand when you host a play-date. Since younger toddlers usually don't play well together, be prepared to keep each entertained individually. Older toddlers can become quite possessive; a well-stocked toy chest may prevent battles. If you are the host and your son has a toy he's especially attached to, put it away before the other child arrives.

Keep it casual. A playdate is a socializing opportunity for toddlers, not a chance for parents to entertain. It's nice to be gracious to the other parent, but the focus should be on the children.

Let the toddlers set the pace. On a first visit, the little ones may do nothing but cling to their parents or whine to leave. It may take several playdates before they feel comfortable. Look for activities such as reading and building with blocks that you can do with both children. Sharing an experience with you is a good way to introduce toddlers to the mechanics of sharing with peers.

Prepare older children. If you have older children at home, tell them that their younger sibling is going to have a visitor and be clear about their role in the event. A child aged four or older can often play very well with toddlers, but don't expect an older child to babysit. Even if an older child is present, never leave toddlers without adult supervision.

Reciprocate. The best thanks you can give to a parent or caregiver who hosts your child on a playdate is to issue a similar invitation for the earliest convenient time.

❦

When to Correct Others' Kids

QUESTION: What should I do when a child is rude and his parents aren't there?

ANSWER: If you know the child well, it's okay to make a simple correction or give an explanation, as long as you do it in a way that doesn't embarrass the child or criticize his parents. It would be fine to say, "Kyle, we don't use language like that in our house." If the child happens to be your grandchild, and it's just the two of you, you might say, "It's so much nicer if you chew with your mouth closed, Rebecca." You don't need to mention the behavior to the child's parents unless it's especially disruptive or outlandish. If the child's parents are present and don't say or do anything about rude behavior, it's best to bite your tongue. If you feel compelled to say something, say it pleasantly: "I really don't appreciate the way you're speaking to me. Could you use a nicer tone?" Model the manners that he should be using.

"IN OUR HOUSE, WE DO IT THIS WAY . . ."

Your child is perfectly mannered, but when his friends come to visit, you're treated to behavior that would rival that in the animal kingdom. Must you go along to get along? Absolutely not. You don't want to be known as the "mean mom," but you can establish guidelines for what's acceptable behavior in your home.

TABLE MANNERS

Your daughter's friends prefer to eat with their fingers, not forks. Should you make them use their silverware, or not bother?

- Don't criticize their eating style.
- Say, "In our house, chicken is a 'fork' food. Can you please use a fork, too? Thanks!"
- Don't try to teach manners to your young guests—that is their parents' responsibility—but you have the right to set expectations for behavior in your own household, whether it's using utensils or choosing G-rated movies.

GENERAL MANNERS

The same guidelines apply for additional kid behavior:

- Picking up toys
- Treating furniture, toys, and belongings with respect
- Observing curfews
- Curbing bad language

In all cases, the operative parent phrase is "In our house . . ."

✳

Responding—or Not—to Rude Comments About Adoption

QUESTION: We adopted our only child three years ago, when she was one. She's of a different race, and I'm shocked by the rude comments people make. The other day we ran into a friend whom I hadn't seen in years who asked me, "Whose little girl is this?" When I answered that she's my daughter, she asked if I have any children of my own! I try not to get upset, but my daughter's old enough to understand what people say, and I worry about her feelings.

ANSWER: Your friend obviously spoke without thinking, and there's little you can do except hold your temper and make a polite reply (something like, "No, we don't have other children. Julia's our only child and our greatest joy"). Your daughter's feelings are your most important concern. You can't shield her from tactless people, but you and your spouse can be good role models for responding to others' ignorance and lack of common sense.

You may be able to cut off most thoughtless remarks by introducing your daughter as soon as you meet people unfamiliar with your family: "I'd like you to meet our daughter, Julia." Change the subject if someone persists with inappropriate remarks or questions. If that doesn't work, you may have to explain that matters such as your child's background or why you chose interracial adoption are personal and not open to discussion.

ADOPTION ETIQUETTE

Children who are adopted have exactly the same status as biological children and should always be treated as such. The following pointers, gathered from adoptive families, will help guide other family members, friends, and acquaintances:

Wait for the parents or child to discuss their personal adoption story. Just as it would be thoughtless to ask about a biological child's conception and birth, it's rude to ask for the details of individual adoptions (for example, whether the adopting parents were present at the birth of a child). The choice to share personal information is theirs—the parents' or the child's—alone.

Don't ask about a child's biological parents. This is a private matter and shouldn't be broached by others. If the adoptive parents raise the subject, it's okay to discuss it, but be careful to use the right term. Birth parents, biological parents, and genetic parents are all correct, but use whatever label the family seems to prefer in conversation. Be sure to avoid the phrase "real parents," which implies that adoptive parents are not real.

Adoptive parents aren't saints. Adoptive parents want children for the same reasons that biological parents do. When others imply that adoptive parents are unusually selfless or have somehow "saved" a child, the results can be to place an especially heavy burden on the parents and create feelings of guilt in the adopted child.

The adoption process can be long and disappointing. Respect the feelings of adopting parents as they cope with the stresses of adopting a child. Unless you've been there, don't be too quick to give advice or to criticize the system. If the adoption falls through, the parents will need time to grieve. A comment such as "You can always try again" trivializes their loss. Instead, recognize that the adopting parents are grieving and offer your support.

Restless in Restaurants

QUESTION: My daughter is seven and has good table manners at home, but when we eat at a restaurant or a relative's house, she's a different child. She wiggles in her chair, talks too loudly, and gulps her food. I have to keep correcting her, which annoys everyone else. Should we just stop going out until she's older?

ANSWER: No. Your daughter needs to experience eating out in order to learn polite behavior. Like most seven-year-olds, she still has trouble with self-restraint; her behavior probably reflects her excitement and nervousness in a different environment. It's also difficult for children her age to sit still very long, so try to keep the outings as brief as possible. You could take her to some "practice" eating-out meals at family-style restaurants or diners—just the two of you or your family. Focus the conversation and instruction on restaurant behavior without embarrassing her. Since children are easily embarrassed, correcting your daughter in front of others will only increase the tension. Try working out a nonverbal signal or two that will let her know when her behavior is out of line. For example, put a finger to your lips when she needs to quiet down. After the outing, talk to her about her behavior. Acknowledge the good and the bad. Before future restaurant visits, let her know that you expect her to use her best "home" manners.

EATING OUT WITH KIDS:
A SURVIVAL GUIDE

Plan ahead. Before going, prep your child. Tell him that he'll be
given a menu, the waiter will take his order, and everyone will
stay at the table until the meal ends. Select a place where you'll
be finished reasonably quickly. When you call to make the reservation, or before you're seated, tell the hostess or manager
that you're dining with kids and would like to be seated near
other families, or away from quiet couples.

Bring quiet toys. Since most young kids aren't used to sitting and
waiting for their meals, bring crayons and a coloring book, or other quiet playthings (without lots of pieces!), to keep your child occupied. Just be sure to put everything away when the food arrives.

Order ASAP. Don't delay putting in your order. For efficiency's
sake, order for any child who's five or under. Be sure your child
knows what he wants before the waiter starts to take your order.

Take a time-out. If a toddler gets restless or noisy, take a break and
escort him from the dining area. Explore the surrounding areas;
just be sure not to distract other diners or the restaurant staff.

Stay seated. Remind children to sit in their chairs. If they run near
servers carrying heavy, scalding-hot dishes, they risk harming
themselves and others.

Clean up spills. If your child makes a mess, do the best you can to
help clean it up. The less you involve the busboy and waiter, the
less you delay service for other diners. Because cleanup will be
more time-consuming than usual, be generous to the waitstaff
with both your appreciation and your tip.

Be considerate of other diners. If your child starts bothering other diners—say, by kicking the back of a booth—put a stop to it pronto. If the diner beats you to the punch, apologize and say that it won't happen again. Then take pains to see that it doesn't.

Know when to go. Children weren't designed to sit still for long periods, and it's unrealistic to expect them to. Unless the service is extremely quick, pass on the dessert and coffee.

✻

9

Let's Eat!

Napkins, Front and Center

QUESTION: Where is the napkin placed, to the left of the place setting or in the center of the plate?

ANSWER: For a formal table setting, the napkin is placed in the center of the place setting, either on the service plate (charger) or on the dinner plate, with the monogram, if any, facing the diner. The napkin is placed on the left side of the place setting if a first course is already on the table when guests are seated; it's preferable to have the open folds of the napkin facing out, to the left. At an informal place setting, the napkin is either to the left of the forks or in the center of the place setting (it need not be on a plate).

ALL SET FOR DINNER

- Start with a clean tablecloth or place mats and coordinating napkins. Napkins go in the center of the place settings or to the left of the forks. Utensils should not be placed on top of the napkin.

- For very formal dinners, the host sets a charger, or service plate, upon which the first course plate is placed. When the first course is cleared, the service plate remains until the entrée plate is served, at which point the two plates are exchanged.

- Set the utensils in the order they'll be used. Starting on the left side of the plate and working from the outside in, set the salad or appetizer fork, then the entrée fork. If salad will be served after the entrée, then the salad fork goes to the right of the entrée fork.

- To the right of the plate, working in, place the soupspoon (if soup will be served), a teaspoon (if coffee is served during the meal), and then the entrée knife. The cutting edge of the knife blade faces the plate. If you're serving a seafood appetizer, the seafood fork (also known as a shellfish or an oyster fork) is placed to the right of the spoon(s) and the knife—the only fork set on the right side of the place setting.

- Traditionally, dessert spoons and forks are brought out before dessert is served. These days, the dessert utensils are often set horizontally above the place setting before the meal. Set the dessertspoon with the handle facing right. Place the dessert fork underneath the spoon with the handle facing left.

- Traditionally, there shouldn't be more than three of any utensil on the table simultaneously.

- The butter plate is placed to the left of the place setting, above the forks. Lay the butter knife diagonally across it.

- When you serve salad on a salad plate, the plate goes to the left of the forks.

- Glasses go directly above the knives and utensils on the right side. Arrange them by size, left to right, starting with the largest—the water goblet—on the far left, followed by the red-wine glass and then the white-wine glass (if wine is being served). Iced tea and other beverages are usually placed to the right of the water glass.

- If you are serving coffee or hot tea, the cup and saucer go just above and slightly to the right of the knife and spoons. At a formal meal, the cup and saucer are brought to the table after the entrée and placed on the right side in the same spot.

Cheers! You've set a beautiful table.

"There's a Fly in My Soup!"

QUESTION: I was a guest at a small dinner party last week and found a hair in my helping of rice casserole. I couldn't bring myself to eat even a bite of the dish. The hostess must have noticed my untouched food. Should I have told her the reason once we were in private?

ANSWER: You did the right thing by not calling attention to the problem. Pointing it out to the hostess, whether in private or not, would embarrass her, and there's nothing she could do about it after the fact. If you discover a foreign object after you've taken a bite, spit it discreetly onto your fork or spoon and put it on the side of your plate. Then, you can continue eating or pass up that particular dish if you like.

FENDING OFF DINNER DISASTERS

Spilled wine, coughing fits, spoiled meat—unexpected problems can crop up at any dinner table. With a few guidelines, as well as a calm demeanor and a sense of humor, you can manage any of these challenges gracefully:

Spills. If you spill food on the table while taking it from a serving dish, neatly pick up as much as you can with a clean spoon or the blade of your knife. Then wet a corner of your napkin in your water glass and dab the spot. If you knock over a drink, quickly set the glass upright and apologize to your tablemates: "I'm sorry! I hope none of it got on you." Get a cloth or sponge and mop up the liquid right away. In a restaurant, discreetly signal the server, who will put a napkin over any stains. In someone's home, immediately tell your host, and help with the cleanup.

Food that's too hot, or spoiled. If a bite of food is too hot, quickly take a swallow of water or another cold drink. If that's impossible or doesn't help, quickly remove the scalding food with your utensil (preferably not with your fingers and not into your napkin), and put it on the edge of the plate. The same goes for a bad oyster or clam, or any food that tastes spoiled: Remove it from your mouth as quickly and unobtrusively as you can.

Wayward food. Food caught in your teeth? Running your tongue over your front teeth is a good way to check for food and the simplest way to clear it off if it's not really lodged in there. If you can't dislodge the food with your tongue, excuse yourself and remove it in the restroom. If you notice food stuck in a fellow diner's teeth or food on her face or clothes, she'll appreciate your telling her. If only the two of you are at the table, say, "Maggie, you seem to have a little something on your chin"; if you're in a group, silently signal her by catching her eye and lightly tapping your chin with your forefinger.

Coughing, sneezing, and nose blowing. When you feel a sneeze or cough coming on, cover your mouth and nose with a handkerchief or tissue—or your napkin, if that's the only thing within reach. In an emergency, your hand is better than nothing at all.

If you can't seem to stop coughing or sneezing, excuse yourself until it passes. If your problem is nose blowing, excuse yourself and blow your nose in the restroom, being sure to wash your hands afterward.

Choking. If you choke on a bit of food, and a sip of water doesn't take care of the problem, cover your mouth and dislodge the morsel with a good cough. If you have to cough more than once or twice, excuse yourself and leave the table. Serious choking is another matter. If you are unable to cough or speak, do whatever's necessary—gesture, grab an arm—to get fellow diners to help. Thankfully, many people, and most restaurant personnel, are trained to perform the life-saving Heimlich Maneuver.

Passing to the Right

QUESTION: When eating family-style, which way should food be passed?

ANSWER: This question is asked of The Emily Post Institute a lot! Technically, food is passed around the table in a counterclockwise direction, or to the right. The reason there's even a guideline for this is to provide some sense of order when passing food. Common sense comes into play here, too. If someone only a few places away from you on your left asks for something to be passed, by all means just pass it to the left instead of sending it all the way around to the right. In general, what's important is that when several dishes are being passed at the same time, they all go in the same direction.

TOP DINNER-TABLE MANNERS GOOFS

- Chewing with your mouth open or talking with food in your mouth
- Slurping, smacking, blowing your nose, or making any unpleasant noises
- Holding your utensil like a shovel or a weapon
- Picking your teeth at the table—or, even worse, flossing
- Not placing your napkin on your lap or not using it at all

- Taking a sip of a drink while still chewing food (unless you're choking)
- Cutting up all your food at once
- Slouching over your place setting or leaning on your elbows while eating
- Executing the "boardinghouse reach" rather than asking someone to pass you something
- Leaving the table without saying "excuse me"

Lipstick at the Table?

QUESTION: I was having lunch with a few good friends at an expensive restaurant recently, and toward the end of the meal I applied some lipstick. One of my friends gave me loads of grief for pulling out my lipstick at the table. I say I was right . . . or was I?

ANSWER: You were right—almost. It's okay to quickly apply lipstick at the table if you're with close friends or relatives, in a non-business situation, and at a non-deluxe restaurant. In general, personal grooming should be done in private for the simple reasons that it can be annoying and it's tacky. But putting on lipstick without the use of a mirror, quickly and without fanfare, is one grooming ritual that can sometimes be performed in front of others. Still, think first! When in doubt, don't do it, such as when you're at a business meal or with people you don't know well.

1. ZIG-ZAG OR CONTINENTAL?

There are two techniques for using your knife and fork: the American style (in which the diner cuts food with the knife in his right hand the fork in his left hand and then switches the fork to his right hand to bring the cut food to his mouth) and the continental style (in which the fork always stays in the left hand and the right hand holds the knife for cutting food). Some Americans are turned off by the continental style, saying it's pretentious. Nonsense. The same could be said of the American style, which Emily Post called "zig-zag" eating: "Why an able-bodied person should like to pretend that the left hand is paralyzed and cannot be lifted more than three of four inches above the table is beyond understanding." The bottom line? Either method is fine. Do what feels comfortable to you.

2. ELBOWS ON THE TABLE?

For a long time, the ironclad rule was **no elbows on the table**. The real issue is how to sit at a table and not look like a slob. If you sit hunched over your plate, leaning on your elbows, and shoveling food into your mouth, then the "no elbows on the table" rule is only one of your problems. In addition to being a gross eater, your slumped position would make you look like you didn't want to be there. All of the above translates into being disrespectful to the others at the table with you.

Yet, sometimes it's actually okay to rest your elbows on the table. That's when you're not really eating—either between courses or before or after the meal—and you need to lean a little toward your fellow diners so that you may hear them. Here, it's fine to gently prop your elbow on the edge of the table; you're polite because you are showing interest in your dinner partners. Use common sense and some caution. An elbow resting gently on the table between courses shouldn't offend anyone—as long as you don't go overboard and start to slump.

3. WHAT'S A CHARGER?

QUESTION: Recently when shopping for new china, I saw what was called a charger. What is it and how is it used?

ANSWER: This large plate, also called a service plate, is on the table as part of the place setting. The charger serves as an underplate for the plate holding the first course, which is brought to the table. When the first course is cleared, the charger (service plate) remains until the plate holding the entrée is served, at which point the two plates are exchanged. Originally, the charger was carefully used at formal meals to ensure that the diner always had a plate in front of him. By keeping the charger at the place setting, followed by the entrée plate, there would be no vacant space in front of the diner. These days, chargers have experienced a comeback as a kind of novelty at many different types of settings, in-cluding informal meals. They are by no means necessary, so don't feel compelled to add them to your china collection unless you really want to. If you do, then have fun with the variety of today's chargers and the more casual ways of using and removing them. In all but the most formal meals, for example, you may certainly remove the charger from a place setting well before the entrée is served.

✳

How to Eat a Cherry Tomato

QUESTION: When eating a cherry tomato, are you supposed to cut it with a knife? I'm afraid of creating a mess.

ANSWER: Cherry tomatoes are tiny, but they sure can squirt! As hors d'oeuvres, they aren't a problem—just pick one up and chew with sealed lips. If they are in a salad, gently prick the skin with your fork before popping one whole in your mouth if it's small, or before carefully cutting it in half.

"IS THAT YOUR BREAD PLATE OR MINE?"

There's a story about Emily Post and table manners that people love to hear. While dining with a group of notable ladies, Emily was asked by one of them at the end of the meal: "Why, Mrs. Post, do you know that you've been eating from my bread plate the entire meal?" Emily's reply? "Well! Isn't that just like me!" Not one to rise to rudeness, Emily's response also relayed her philosophy—that etiquette is based on the principles of honesty (with tact!), respect, and consideration. Etiquette is a code of behavior that we follow to make those around us feel comfortable. Emily did not commit the major breach of etiquette in this situation; her dining partner made the breach by pointing out Emily's mistake. Don't highlight someone's mistake; rise above it in order to make those around you feel welcome. Oh, and by the way, your bread plate is the one on your left—slightly above your forks. It just so happens that your salad plate is over there, too, to the left of your forks.

10

"Reservations, Please"

Eager Eater

QUESTION: When I'm eating out with a group and some of the meals are served before others, is it okay to start eating, or should I wait until everyone is served?

ANSWER: If a noticeable amount of time elapses after the arrival of some meals and before the arrival of others, then the host, or other diners, should encourage those who have already been served to go ahead and eat. This particular etiquette tidbit applies to meals that are to be served (and eaten) hot. If everyone has ordered cold food, those served first should wait until everyone has their meals before starting to eat.

COMMON DINING DILEMMAS

You don't like the food. Send a dish back only if it isn't what you ordered, has not been prepared the way you requested (a "medium-well" steak arrives raw, for instance), tastes spoiled, or contains a hair or a pest. Speak calmly and discreetly to the server when making your request.

You want to taste a companion's food. Accepting another's offer to taste some of his dish—or offering a bite of yours—is fine as long as it's done subtly and neatly. Pass your bread plate to the person so he can put a spoonful on it; or, if he's sitting close by, hold your plate toward him so that he can put a bit on it. Do not hold a forkful of food to another diner's mouth or spear something off his plate—both moves are messy and unappetizing.

Your side dishes are served on separate plates. It's fine to eat vegetables or other side dishes directly from an individual plate if the item is for you alone. If you prefer to transfer the food to your dinner plate, use a utensil or carefully slide it onto the dish. You could also ask your server to transfer the side dish to your plate and remove the empty dish so that the table isn't overcrowded.

You're faced with unfamiliar foods. When a platter arrives with food that you aren't sure how to eat—an unusual type of sushi, perhaps, or crab in the shell—you can (1) wait until someone else starts to eat and follow suit; (2) ask how the food should be eaten—"with fingers or forks?" (3) avoid the food altogether. Crying out, "Ewww . . . what's that?" is not an option.

You're not sure what to do with your utensils. Never place a fork or spoon you've been using directly on the table. (Note: This applies even if a server asks you "to place your soiled utensils for the next course.") Instead, place the utensil diagonally on your plate, not propped against it like an oar. If you place your knife and fork in a position where they are pointing toward each other in an upside-down V shape, it's a signal to your server that you're just pausing to speak or take a drink; if you lay them side by side diagonally on your plate, you're ready for the server to remove your plate.

✳

It's an Order: Don't Hold Back

QUESTION: I like to entertain in restaurants but find that ordering is often awkward, as some guests don't seem to know what to get. How can I let them know that they can order anything they want?

ANSWER: Sometimes guests are afraid to order something too expensive or are concerned that they'll be the only one ordering an appetizer or soup. It's incumbent upon the host to put everyone at ease by saying things like, "The chilled shrimp are the best I've ever had, and the Caesar salad is a must if you're a fan [so they know it's okay to order a first course], and I can also recommend the prime rib [or another item that is in the top price range]." Without your having to say, "Please order an appetizer," you'll let guests know that you expect them to do so, and that they don't have to seek out the least expensive entrée item, either.

RESTAURANT HOST WITH THE MOST

Consider your guests' tastes. If possible, find out whether your guests especially like or dislike certain foods or ethic cuisines. You can ask when extending the invitation or give them a choice of two or three restaurants. If you're hosting a group, choose a restaurant with a wide-ranging menu so everyone can find something to his or her taste. Think about convenience and logistics, too.

Choose a restaurant you know. Even a popular new place with the hottest chef in town may have snail-like service or be so noisy or cramped that it's hard to carry on a conversation. Go with the sure bet.

Reserve a table ahead of time. You may not mind sitting at the bar waiting for a table, but others in your party might.

Arrive early. Get there a few minutes before your guests. This will relieve them of the worry of whether they should go ahead to the table if they arrive first. If you wait at the table, give the maitre d' the names of the guests and ask him to direct them to you. If you wait in the foyer for several guests and some are more than ten minutes late, go ahead and be seated, asking the maitre d' to show tardy guests to the table.

Stand for latecomers. If a latecomer arrives after you're seated, stand as you extend your greeting.

Get things started on a good note. Be sure to introduce all of your guests to one another, after you've greeted each one individually. Whether you order a pre-meal drink or not, make it clear that your guests may order drinks, and of any sort, if they wish.

Encourage everyone to dig in. If the meals arrive at different times, urge those who've already been served to go ahead and start eating, especially if they have hot food.

"Check, please." When paying the check, don't display or disclose the total. Even a joking "Well, it's a good thing we enjoyed our food" could make guests feel they've ordered too extravagantly. If you're a woman, make it clear to the maitre d' or manager (either call ahead or mention upon your arrival) that the check is to be presented to you and you alone—not to one of the men in the group. Some women also pay before the meal begins, to avoid confusion over who pays.

Waiting in the Wings

QUESTION: I was recently invited to lunch with a business associate. I arrived before he did and had the restaurant staff seat me. Should I have waited for my host?

ANSWER: In business settings, it's best to wait for the host in the lobby or waiting area rather than at the table. That will allow him to take the lead when he arrives. If you're the host, wait for your guest in the lobby rather than at the table, too, if you can. However, if the restaurant is filling up and the staff tells you that you need to be seated in order to hold your table, it's okay to do so. This applies whether you're the guest or the host. The maitre d' will direct the other person to your table when he arrives. For a social meeting with friends, it's fine to be seated if you arrive first—regardless of how full the restaurant is getting.

THE GOOD RESTAURANT GUEST

- Never complain to the maitre d' about the choice of table, no matter how much you dislike the location. The host alone should request a switch.

- When ordering a drink, try to stay more or less in line with what everyone else is ordering. In a free-spirited group, tequila shots may not raise an eyebrow. But they're a bad idea if everyone else is having iced tea, fruit juice, and club soda.

- When your host orders a drink at a meal with a time limit (a business lunch or a pre-theater dinner, for example), order at least some kind of beverage so he won't think you're worried about pre-meal drinks slowing things down.

- In general, don't order the most expensive items on the menu. Even if your host says "Please order whatever you want," it's best to stick to the medium-priced range. You can also take your cue from what the others at the table are ordering and then order something that is about the same price. On the other hand, you needn't pick the least expensive foods being offered; that could imply that you think that is all the host can afford.

- Send food back only if there's something wrong with it, not because you've decided you don't like it.

- Never complain about the food or service. Sounding dissatisfied could make it appear that you question the host's taste in restaurants.

- Even if the host has tipped the coat-check person because he collected all the tickets on arrival, it's a nice gesture to try to reimburse him: "Jack, won't you please let me take care of this?" But also know when to take no for an answer.

- Be appreciative: Whether it's a business meal or strictly social, always thank your host. Do so at least once, in person, at the end of the meal. Then, follow up promptly with a short handwritten thank-you note—the best and warmest way to go (and a must in many business scenarios such as after a job interview over a meal)—or via a phone call or email.

Chipping Away at the Tip

QUESTION: If I get lousy service in a restaurant, is it okay to withhold the tip?

ANSWER: Reducing the tip is okay; eliminating it is not. A good rule of thumb is to tip ten percent if the service is mediocre and eight percent if it's really poor. But going any lower than eight percent is too harsh. (Restaurant servers pay taxes on eight percent above their straight take-home pay, so to cut back on tips below that amount is extremely drastic and often unfair). Keep in mind that a small tip does not correct the problem (often not the server's fault anyway). A small tip simply hurts all the employees sharing on the tip pool—and the others may have given you good service. Leaving no tip at all is also ambiguous. The server may think you forgot, or stiffed him, and your point will be lost. Cutting back on the tip sends a clear message that the service was not satisfactory. It's a good idea to speak (discreetly) with the restaurant manager about any problems so that they can be addressed.

If you're experiencing problems during a restaurant meal, don't wait until you pay to express yourself. Tell your server or the restaurant manager immediately and give him a chance to rectify the problem. If he does, tip the full amount (fifteen to twenty percent is customary). If the problem isn't resolved, or your server doesn't work hard enough to resolve it, then you can reduce the tip.

TIPPING GUIDELINES

- *A tip should always be earned.* Reward good service generously and reduce the tip proportionately for indifferent or rude service. That way, you help to raise the standard of service.

- *Treat servers with respect.* Leaving a generous tip doesn't make up for ordering someone around or treating them dismissively. While tipping augments servers' incomes and rewards them for a job well done, treating them kindly is just as important.

- *When in doubt about whether to tip, ask in advance.* If a department store is scheduled to deliver a new sofa, call and ask someone in the furniture department whether tipping is customary; in a hair salon, ask the receptionist. In some situations, leaving a tip could be seen as demeaning. Taking the time to find out what's expected can spare you an embarrassing moment.

- *Tip on the pre-tax amount of the bill, not on the total.*

- *Tip discreetly.* Tipping is a private matter. Don't act like a "big spender" and flash a lot of bills.

- *Money is the tip of choice.* Sometimes a small gift, usually given during the holidays, can be substituted for cash. In the case of a hairdresser, for example, this gift can "top off" the cash tips you've given over the year.

�֍

11

Out and About

New Low: Bathroom Stall as Phone Booth

QUESTION: I was in the bathroom at a restaurant and the woman in the stall next to me was talking on her cell phone! I was forced to listen to her conversation, while others waited in line for a stall. Was there anything I could have done?

ANSWER: Is no place sacred? You'd think you'd be safe from intrusive cell phone conversations in the bathroom! Someone who makes a call there is invading your privacy by forcing you to listen in. Not to mention that she's hogging the stall! There's nothing much you can do about such boorish behavior while in the stall next door, but upon leaving the restroom you *could* tell the restaurant manager about the problem. I think restaurants should post notices declaring restrooms cell phone–free zones. In the meantime, cell phone users, listen up: When the urge to make a call strikes, take it outside.

THE TOP FIVE CELL PHONE TURNOFFS

Talking Too Loudly

Whenever you make a call in public, speak as quietly as you can. Don't shout into your phone. Talking loudly forces everyone around you to listen in, try as they might to tune you out.

Leaving the Ringer On in Quiet Places

Theaters, places of worship, and funerals should always be cell phone–free zones—as should most enclosed spaces (like public restrooms) where you can't maintain a ten-foot distance from other people. Turn the ringer off and let the phone take messages until you're in a place where you can talk freely without disturbing anyone. If you must be "on call" for some reason, leave the phone in vibrate mode and move quietly to answer it where you won't disturb anyone.

Ignoring Those You're With

Live people should get priority over disembodied voices. If you want your friends or relatives to feel second-rate—is that what you want to do?!—then make or take calls when you're in the middle of a conversation with them. (If your sudden call is an emergency, however, go for it; in this case, they'll understand.)

Going on a Calling Jag in Public

Keep calls to a minimum on public transportation, in line at the bank, store, or movies, or in busy areas like airports. Placing one call after another (especially just to pass the time) eventually exasperates even the most understanding captive listener. Barring an emergency, limit your calls or move to a more private spot.

Using Offensive Language

If you must inflict your conversation on others, don't add insult to injury by using obscenities or telling gross stories (". . . and so, my surgery went like this . . .").

✳

Gabbing at the Gym

QUESTION: My friend goes to the gym at the same time that I go. She gets on the treadmill next to me and starts blabbing away. I want peace and quiet! How should I tell her?

ANSWER: For many of us, the gym is a private refuge from stress. Tell your friend that as much as you enjoy her company, at the gym you need to concentrate on exercising. Then suggest getting together sometime after the workout, so she doesn't feel rejected.

FITNESS CENTER ETIQUETTE

- Wipe your sweat off mats and machines. No one wants to sit or lie in someone else's perspiration. Carry a towel for this purpose, or use disinfectant spray and wipes if supplied by the gym.
- Don't leave weights and dumbbells on a bar or machine. Otherwise, the next person who uses the equipment may have to spend time removing them.
- Don't hog the weight machines. When others want to use them, agree to rotate your sets.
- If all the treadmills or any other cardio machines are taken, limit

your time to give those who may be waiting a chance. Many gyms limit time on popular machines at peak periods.

- If you like to flirt, don't be a pest. Save it for elsewhere. If you try to strike up a conversation with someone you find attractive and they give you the brush-off (no matter how politely), drop your overture then and there.
- A quick and friendly "hello" is one thing, but chatting with someone while they're working out could interrupt their routine.
- Comply with the fitness center's rules, such as wearing correct workout shoes (black soles can be a problem), not using cell phones, and signing in at the front desk.
- Be odor-aware: Arrive clean, remember to apply deodorant, and lay off the perfume and cologne.
- Be punctual for personal training sessions and group fitness classes.
- Do your part to keep the fitness area neat and safe: Keep your towels, water bottles, and fitness logs with you at all times so they're out of the way of others.
- Keep your clothes and other personal items stored in a locker. Clean up after yourself in the locker room's showers and changing areas. Deposit used towels in their receptacles.

�֍

Flying the Un-Friendly Skies

QUESTION: I'm fed up with parents who let their children act up on airplanes. During my last few flights, I've been kicked, poked, and tormented with nonstop whining and tantrums. How do I make it stop?

ANSWER: Unless you can afford a private jet or a quiet first-class seat, kids are part of the air travel package. Parents should certainly try to keep their children quiet, and many do. Confront those who don't at your own risk, since embarrassing the parents of a crying or misbehaving child will only add more stress to the situation. The first tactic to try is avoidance: Leave your seat and see if a vacant one is available. If not, try earplugs (keep them in your carry-on or ask the flight attendant for a pair). You could ask a flight attendant to do something about the problem. (Sometimes, they're able to resolve things, but don't count on it.) Or, politely tell young seat-kickers or their parents: "Excuse me, but my seat is being kicked." With any luck, the parent (or child) will apologize and put a stop to this particular form of in-flight torture.

TOP FLIGHT FAUX PAS

Annoying behavior becomes excruciating when people are wedged into an aluminum tube for hours on end. Problems even pop up before and after the flight. Here are some common discourtesies to avoid:

Dumping on flight attendants. Keep your requests reasonable and say "please" and "thank you;" flight attendants are not servants. Treating them decently also means they'll be more willing to help you out if you need a favor.

Loud conversations. Broadcasting your weekend plans to all within earshot or chatting loudly with other passengers is obnoxious. So is blocking the aisles and hovering over innocent passengers to schmooze with your friends. Turn down your volume and keep the aisles clear.

Overdoing the booze. Alcohol hits harder at high altitudes, so it's not surprising that drunk passengers are often behind instances of "air rage." Skip the cocktail, or drink in moderation if you must, and you'll also be in better shape for whoever, or whatever, awaits you when you land.

Smelly situations. Strong odors are another cruel way to torment your seatmates. Too much perfume can be as hard to take as bad BO. If you must bring food on board, don't make it a sausage-garlic sub. Change the baby's stinky diaper in the bathroom, not at your seat. And, please, don't remove your shoes so your feet can get some air.

Pushing onto and off of the plane. No bullying your way through
the aisle in a mad dash to your assigned seat or to the exit
when the plane has landed. And use caution not to knock other
passengers with your luggage (pay extra attention to any back-
packs and shoulder bags). Remember to say "Excuse me" or "I'm
sorry" if you bump someone.

Tipping Airport Porters

QUESTION: My elderly uncle is coming for a visit, traveling alone by airplane. I've arranged for someone to meet him with a wheel-chair at the gate and bring him to me in the baggage area. Should I tip this person?

ANSWER: Yes, you should; anything from $2 to $5 would be good—and customary. If the attendant goes the extra mile by, say, pushing the wheelchair from one end of the airport to the other, give at the high end of the range.

WHO TO TIP AT THE HOTEL

Doorman

Takes luggage from your vehicle to the front desk; hails you a cab and opens the door, particularly at luxury hotels.

Tip: $1 to $2 for carrying luggage; $1 to $4 for getting a taxi (the higher end if it's raining or if the doorman had trouble flagging down a cab); none required for opening the door.

Front-Desk Clerk

Checks you in and out and can also provide help with very brief requests, such as for directions and information about the city.

Tip: None required.

Bellhop

Takes your luggage from the front desk to your room; also runs errands like delivering faxes and packages to your door.

Tip: $1 to $2 per bag, depending on the quality of the hotel, but not less than $2 total; $2 to $3 for running an errand for you.

Concierge

Provides an array of services, from giving directions to making dinner reservations, particularly at luxury hotels.

Tip: None required for answering a question; $5 to $10 (immediately, not upon checkout) for each special service; more for miraculous efforts like obtaining tickets to a sold-out show.

Housekeeper

Makes the beds, changes the towels, cleans the room and bathroom, and sometimes turns down sheets.

Tip: $2 per day in a moderate hotel, $3 to $5 per day in a deluxe hotel. Leaving a daily tip in the room rather than when you check out ensures that the tip will go to the specific person who cleaned your room that day.

Valet

Parks and retrieves your car.

Tip: $2 to $3 per handoff.

Room-Service Waiter

Delivers food to your room at hotels that have restaurants.

Tip: Fifteen to twenty percent of the total charge. Check the bill to see if the gratuity has already been included (it usually is for room service). But don't confuse this tip (it is identified as "gratuity") with a "delivery charge." The delivery charge is not the same; the server does not receive any of this charge.

Bed-and-Breakfast Owner

Usually serves as cook, housekeeper, and tour guide for guests—who are generally treated more like friends and family. Sometimes, guests enjoy their stay so much and receive such attentive service that they thank the B&B owner(s) with a note and small gift.

Tip: None required for the owners. If there are any B&B employees (housekeeper, bellhop, waitstaff in the dining room), they should be tipped the same as hotel employees.

12

It's Party Time!

Vegetarian Options

QUESTION: I'm a vegetarian. When I'm invited to a dinner party, should I tell this to the host ahead of time? What about my wife, who's allergic to certain foods?

ANSWER: Definitely mention any allergy that could cause a serious reaction. When you call to RSVP, explain to your host, "We'd love to come for dinner, but I have to tell you that Becky is deathly allergic to peanuts." Dietary preferences such as vegetarianism or a low-carb diet should be handled differently. At large parties and buffets, where there's usually a large variety of foods to choose from, make do with what's available. However, if the gathering is small, the dinner is in your honor, or you're going to be an overnight houseguest, do mention your restrictions and offer to bring a dish to share. Say, "Thanks so much for the invitation. I should let you know that I'm a vegetarian. I'd love to bring a quiche if that's okay with you." This way, your host won't waste time preparing the wrong food for you or have to trouble himself figuring out what type of dish would best suit your preferences.

THE GOOD GUEST'S BIBLE

Even for the most casual parties, these basics of politeness should be automatic:

RSVP. Immediately. If you delay your reply, you complicate the host's planning and make it seem as if you're waiting for something better to come along. Even if no RSVP has been requested, it's thoughtful to let your host know whether or not you plan to be there.

Be on time. Punctuality means different things in different locales, but in general, guests should arrive at or shortly after the time stated on the invitation. Typically, "fashionably late" means no more than fifteen minutes late. Being early is actually as bad as being late. Circle the block if you must, but don't surprise your host.

Be a willing participant. When your host says it's time for dinner, head straight for the table. If you're asked to participate in a party game or to view Susie's graduation pictures, accept graciously and enthusiastically (even if you are groaning inwardly).

Offer to help. If you're with the host in the kitchen as he prepares the food, suggest a specific task: "I'd be happy to chop veggies for the salad or fill the water glasses." Even if your offer is refused, the gesture will be appreciated. When the party ends, offer to help with the cleanup.

Don't overindulge. Attacking the finger foods as if you haven't eaten in a week not only is unpleasant to witness but will leave less food for other guests. Keep any consumption of alcoholic beverages light to moderate.

Remember: Neatness counts. This means many things, from not
leaving shrimp tails on the coffee table to not being a slob when
you're an overnight guest.

Thank the host twice. The first thank-you comes at the end of
the party. In some parts of the country, a second thank-you by
phone is customary the next day, a gesture that's gracious any-
where. A written thank-you is in order if the party was formal. In
fact, a written note is *always* appreciated, no matter how casual
the get-together.

Feet First

QUESTION: Is it okay to ask my guests to remove their shoes at the door? The dirt, salt, and mud that people bring in on their shoes are ruining my wood floors and area rugs.

ANSWER: Yes—as long as you're considerate about it. Offer guests slippers or non-skid socks so they won't be cold or embarrassed about showing their feet. Explain it this way: "I hope you won't mind taking off your shoes—it really cuts down on the dirt that gets tracked in this time of year. Please help yourself to a pair of slippers." Be flexible—if you don't know your guests well, or are having a big party, nix the no-shoes policy.

SIX WAYS TO BE
A GOOD HOST

No matter the kind of party, there are some things a host should remember, even before the party starts.

Invite clearly. Include necessary information for your guests in the invitation. Is the party a casual get-together or more formal?

What about the attire? Maybe a guest would benefit by knowing ahead of time who else will be there, which you might mention when he RSVPs.

Plan well. Preparing your guest list carefully is key to a successful party. After the list is set, do as much as you can ahead of time, cleaning and preparing food and refreshments. (Lower the stress level by serving what you know will work.) It's optional, but in advance you might also want to ask a guest whom you don't know very well if he has any food restrictions or allergies. Doing so especially makes sense if he's going to be your only guest, a houseguest, or part of a small party. Get everything ready well before your guests arrive, so you'll feel relaxed from the very beginning.

Remain calm. Giving a party can be enjoyable, especially if you approach it with simplicity. Get help if necessary, and don't let your guests think you're huffing and puffing. They'll feel far more comfortable if they don't have to wonder whether they're causing you trouble.

Keep guests feeling welcome. Make sure guests are warmly greeted—and that the feeling of being welcome is sustained throughout the party. Keep a lookout for each guest's well-being as much as you possibly can. If you notice that a guest has an empty glass or if there's one person standing alone, remedy the situation as quickly and cheerfully as possible.

Be flexible and gracious. Your soufflé flops. Or one friend arrives with an unexpected guest. *The flopped dessert?* Have a fallback. *The uninvited guest?* As discourteous as it is for someone to spring such a surprise on you, be gracious. No polite host would ever send an uninvited guest packing.

Be appreciative. Thank people for coming as you bid them good-bye. And don't forget to say "thank you" to anyone who brought you a gift.

Double-Dipping Dilemma

QUESTION: What's the best way to handle a guest who is double dipping?

ANSWER: If you're the host and know the offender well, discreetly and politely—but firmly—ask the person to stop. If the double dipping seems to have just begun, remove the dip to the kitchen and spoon out the tainted part. If the dip is beyond redemption, toss it and put out a fresh bowl. If you don't know the double dipper well, keep mum, but discreetly remove the dip and dump it. Then let it go and enjoy the party. If you are a guest at the party, you can whisper in the host's ear about what you've witnessed. And, of course, skip the dip.

A QUICK
CLEANUP

QUESTION: If a guest spills something on my carpet during a party, is it rude to clean it up right away?

ANSWER: It's rude only if you show your guest that you're angry or annoyed. Otherwise, your tackling the cleanup will be a relief to everyone, especially if you make a lighthearted comment, such as, "See, no damage done!" There's nothing rude about a gracious, prompt cleanup.

Grace Under Pressure

QUESTION: It is our family's custom to say grace before meals. Is it okay to say prayers when we have guests for dinner?

ANSWER: Certainly. One of the warmest gestures you can make is to include a dinner guest in a family tradition. The only exception would be if you think it might make most of your guests uncomfortable. But you can usually put guests at ease by quietly assuring them ahead of time that they need not participate. Anyone who is nonreligious, or of a different religion, should just sit quietly during grace. These guests can practice "discreet nonparticipation" in the prayer, while still respecting the beliefs of the host and hostess.

MORE DINING DILEMMAS

QUESTION: Is it polite to ask a guest to do the honor of saying grace, or is it better to say it myself?

ANSWER: It's polite to ask, but do so before everyone is assembled around the table. This gives the guest a chance to decline if he would be uncomfortable saying the prayers, without appearing rude by refusing in front of other guests. It also gives him time to collect his thoughts if he accepts your offer. When a minister or rabbi is among your dinner guests, he should always be asked to say grace. Of course, you should never force anyone to recite a group grace or even say "amen," especially if it's not part of their religious background to do so.

QUESTION: I have a few friends who rarely drink or are recovering alcoholics, as well as those, like myself, who enjoy a cocktail or glass of wine with dinner. Is it okay to mix these two groups, or should I try to entertain them separately?

ANSWER: It's fine to mix drinkers and teetotalers, but be careful not to make the non-drinkers feel conspicuous. Stock up on nonalcoholic beverages, such as soft drinks, water, seltzer, tonic, and fruit juices and serve them just as you normally do. You could also offer garnishes like lemon and lime slices, if you think these would enhance the beverages. Provide alternatives with meals. Most non-drinking guests will want water, but they may also enjoy coffee or iced tea. If you are having champagne, chill a bottle of sparkling grape juice as well. Be considerate about seating arrangements. Your friend in recovery shouldn't have to spend the evening next to a wine enthusiast extolling the virtues of a particular pinot noir.

QUESTION: I'm having a large dinner party and some of my guests have never been to my house. I don't have time to clean the upstairs. What should I do if people ask for a house tour?

ANSWER: Unless your party is a housewarming, you don't need to give a house tour at all. Make it clear that your upstairs is off-limits by turning off hall lights and shutting the doors to all the rooms there. Polite guests know not to open closed doors or enter unlighted areas. If someone asks for a tour, show them your downstairs rooms.

If you see someone wandering into an area where he isn't wanted, divert his attention—"John, we were just heading back to the dining room. Did you get a chance to try the shrimp?"—and usher him back to the party area. You could also be more direct: "Next time, I'll show you the upstairs. For now, though, it's off-limits."

The Disappearing Houseguest

QUESTION: When I'm visiting someone for the weekend, how can I gracefully excuse myself for a while to give us both some space?

ANSWER: As long as you don't do it in the middle of dinner preparations or a planned activity, you'll probably make your hostess's day if you disappear for a bit so she can regroup, take a nap, or simply not feel obligated to entertain you for a while. Just say, "Jenna, all this sea air has wiped me out—would it be all right with you if I took a nap?" Or, "If you don't need me for an hour or two, I think I'll drag out my laptop and tackle that report I have to review." Or, "That hammock looks so inviting—if nobody else has claimed it for the next hour or so, I'd love to try it out with the book I've brought along."

HOW TO BE A WELCOME HOUSEGUEST

1. **NEVER ASK IF YOU CAN BRING YOUR PET.** If you must travel with your pet, ask about a good kennel in the area.

2. **BRING A GIFT AND WRITE A THANK-YOU.** It's fine to send the gift when you get home, or treat your host to a night out instead.

3. **MAKE IT SHORT AND SWEET.** Before your visit, tell your host when you'll arrive and when you'll depart. Take your cues from your host, but a good rule of thumb is to keep your visit to no more than three nights. And stick to your schedule.

4. **PITCH IN.** Make your bed, clean up after yourself, and help in the kitchen—unless your host objects.

5. **BRING YOUR OWN SUPPLIES.** Don't expect the guestroom to be stocked like a five-star hotel. Bring your own shampoo and slippers.

13

Gifts Galore

"Thank You for the Thank-You"

QUESTION: I recently hosted a dinner party. The next day, one of the guests sent me a bouquet of flowers. Do I have to thank her for her thank-you gift?

ANSWER: Yes—to let her know that her gift arrived and that you appreciate her thoughtfulness. The best way to extend your "thanks" is via a handwritten note, although it would also be okay to call or email her instead. If she had brought the flowers to the party, a follow-up thank-you wouldn't be necessary, since you would have had the chance to thank her in person.

TO WRITE, OR NOT TO WRITE, THANK-YOU NOTES?

It's never wrong to send a written thank-you—and people always appreciate getting "thanks" in writing. Why? Handwritten notes are warmer and more special than other forms of thank-yous. The rule of thumb is that you should send a written note any time you receive a gift and the giver wasn't there for you to thank in person. But notes are not always necessary. If, for example, the gift is from a close friend or relative (and it's not a wedding gift) you can email or call instead if you prefer. Below are some other note-writing guidelines:

Shower gifts. Even though the gift giver attended the shower in your honor and you had a chance to say thanks for her gift, you should still send a written note.

Wedding gifts. Each wedding gift should be acknowledged with a written note within three months of receipt of the gift. It's best to write the notes as soon as possible after gifts arrive, however. Write a note even if you've thanked the giver in person.

Congratulatory gifts or cards. Anyone who sends a present, or a card with a personally written message, should receive a note in return.

Gifts received when sick. Thank-you notes should be written as soon as the patient feels well enough—or a friend or relative can write the notes. It's okay to call close friends rather than write.

Condolence notes or gifts. Everyone who has sent a personal note, flowers, or a donation should get a written thank-you. A close friend or relative can write the notes on the recipient's behalf.

❀

When a Gift Is a Dud

QUESTION: My sister-in-law just asked me why I haven't worn the jacket she gave me for my birthday. I dodged the question because I didn't want to tell her that I returned it. What should I say?

ANSWER: When you receive a gift that's not quite right, you have two choices: Grin and bear it, or politely ask the giver if she'll mind if you exchange it. Since you've already acted, now you're stuck. You'll have to tell your sister-in-law what you did. Express your gratitude first, so that you don't hurt her feelings. Say, "Maggie, I loved the color, but the style wasn't right for me. I exchanged it for this blazer. I hope you don't mind."

REDUCE, REUSE, REGIFT?

Since the writers of *Seinfeld* coined the term *regifting* in the 1990s, it has become part of our everyday language—and a hotly debated topic. Is it okay to pass on a gift you've received to someone else? Is it ethical? The answer is a very qualified yes. Regifting can be done, though rarely, and under these very specific circumstances:

- You're certain the gift is something the recipient would enjoy.
- The gift is brand new (no castoffs allowed) and comes with its original box and instructions.
- The gift isn't handmade, or one that the original giver took great care to select.
- Neither your gift giver nor your recipient will be upset.

Simply put, you have to *make sure you don't hurt feelings*— neither the original giver's nor the recipient's. For instance, if you received a set of wineglasses from your sister-in-law that you didn't need, do you think she'd mind if you passed them along to a friend who just bought a house? Do the two women know each other? Would it be awkward if they found out? Is there a chance your friend might need to exchange the glasses for something else herself, and if she asked you where you bought them, what would you tell her? When in doubt, do not regift.

Here are two scenarios where recycling a gift would be appropriate:

- Your sister's coffeemaker just stopped working, and her birthday is days away. You, who are on a budget, were recently given a coffeemaker that's a duplicate of the one you already have. Your sister has always liked yours. Instead of stashing the extra coffeemaker in your closet, you wrap it in its original box and present it to her. She's thrilled.
- You've been given two copies of the same book. Your best friend, with whom you exchange Christmas gifts each year, is a fan of the author. You decide to give her the book as a holiday gift. Or, you may choose to give her the book not as a holiday gift, but as an "I've received an extra" gift: "Jessica, I received two copies of this book and want you to have one." An "unofficial" gift of this kind need not be wrapped.

Only you can decide whether to regift—and how to do it appropriately. Think through each situation carefully, and if you're in doubt, don't do it. A gifting gaffe isn't worth the price of a coffeemaker, for example. You can always keep the item in storage or do a good deed by donating the gift to a nonprofit or shelter, where it would be used and appreciated without ambiguity or hurt feelings.

'Tis the Season to Tip Helpers

QUESTION: Do I really need to give a cash gift to all of the service providers in my life? That would put me in the poorhouse!

ANSWER: No; first and foremost, stick to your budget. Set aside a portion of your holiday budget for tips. Then, select the two or three service providers whose services or personalities you couldn't do without. This list can easily change from year to year. For young families, one of those persons may be the day-care provider or nanny; for others, a housecleaner or massage therapist. Always accompany a cash tip with a brief handwritten note of thanks.

"WHOM SHOULD I TIP AND HOW MUCH?"

During the holiday season it's customary to thank the people, seen and unseen, who help your life run smoothly throughout the year. That "thank you" usually comes in the form of cash. Who should get a tip and how much? The answer varies, depending on

- The quality and frequency of the service
- Your relationship with the service person
- Where you live (amounts are usually higher in large cities)
- How long you've worked together

- Your budget
- Regional customs

If you always tip at the time of service, you can skip the holiday tip or cut back on the amount. Include a handwritten note with the cash—that makes it more personal and is one of the best ways to express appreciation. Tell the provider how pleased you are with what they do for you.

If you're strapped for cash, just be more conservative. Select the two or three people whose services you couldn't live without, and give to them. A small gift or a baked good with a handwritten note of thanks can substitute for a monetary gift.

When selecting gifts for teachers, day-care providers, nannies, and babysitters, have your child write the card, help you pick out the gift, or deliver it. It's an excellent way to teach kids about expressing appreciation.

The tip amounts below are merely guidelines—every situation is different, so let your common sense and holiday spirit be your guide:

AU PAIR	*One week's pay, plus a small gift from your child*
BABYSITTER, REGULAR	*One evening's pay, plus a small gift from your child*
BARBER	*Cost of one haircut, plus possibly a small gift*
BEAUTY SALON STAFF	*$10 to $60 each, giving the most to those who do the most for you, plus possibly a small gift*
CHILD'S TEACHER	*Gift, not cash; check school's policy. Possibilities: gift certificate for coffee shop or bookstore; classroom supplies; book; picture frame; fruit basket or gourmet food item; or joint gift with other parents and children*

DAY-CARE PROVIDERS	$25 to $70 each, plus a small gift from your child. If only one or two providers, consider higher-range amount
DOG WALKER	One week's pay
FITNESS TRAINER, PERSONAL	Cost of one session
GARAGE ATTENDANTS	$10 to $30 each, given to and distributed by manager
HOUSEKEEPER/CLEANER	One day's pay
LETTER CARRIERS	U.S. government regulations permit carriers to accept gifts worth up to $20 each
MASSAGE THERAPIST	One session's fee
NANNY	One week's to one month's salary based on tenure and customs in your area, plus a small gift from your child
NEWSPAPER DELIVERER	$10 to $30
NURSE, PRIVATE	Gift, not cash
NURSING HOME EMPLOYEES	Gifts, not cash
PACKAGE DELIVERER	Small gift if you receive deliveries regularly (most delivery companies prohibit cash gifts)
POOL CLEANER	Cost of one cleaning
RESIDENTIAL BUILDING PERSONNEL	
DOORMAN	$10 to $80
ELEVATOR OPERATOR	$15 to $40
HANDYMAN	$15 to $40
SUPERINTENDENT	$20 to $80
TRASH/RECYCLING COLLECTORS	$10 to $20 each, for private service
YARD AND GARDEN WORKERS	$20 to $50

Breaking the Gift Chain

QUESTION: I've been exchanging Christmas presents for years with a few friends and relatives whom I'm no longer especially close with. I'm trying to simplify things around the holidays. Is there a graceful way to let them know I'd like to bow out?

ANSWER: Yes, and it's not as hard as you think. Just be frank. Long before Christmas, write, call, email, or say to the person, "I've loved your gifts, but with the economy the way it is [or the new baby, or redecorating, or whatever seems like a good reason] why don't we just exchange cards this year? Write us with your family news—that will be the best present of all."

HOW TO SIMPLIFY GIFT GIVING

These tips will help take the hassle out of gift giving—and put the joy back in:

- **Keep a running gift shopping list throughout the year.** Include hints or wish lists from loved ones for their birthday or holiday gifts, as well as your own ideas. Be on the lookout for the items when shopping and browsing catalogs and Web sites.

- **Trust your judgment.** Lose the idea that the gift has to be perfect. If you think the person will like it, they probably will.
- **Stick to your budget.** Spending more than you should takes the fun out of gift giving.
- **Buy it when you see it.** If you're shopping in July and see a sweater that your mother would love for Christmas, grab it. Chances are it won't be there when you look in December.
- **Keep a few emergency gifts stashed in the closet.** Just make sure they're good ones.

14

Wedding Bells

Engaging Presents

QUESTION: I'm invited to a friend's engagement party. Do I need to bring a gift?

ANSWER: In the past, gifts were not expected at an engagement party, and that is often still the case today. However, in some parts of the country, bringing a gift to an engagement party has become de rigueur. If you're unsure whether to bring a gift for the engaged couple, it's perfectly okay to ask the host of the party (or a local wedding planner) about local custom—that is, should you bring a gift or not? Also, some couples prefer to forgo engagement-party gifts even in areas where they're given more often than not, and ask their hosts to inform guests about "no gifts" when the RSVPs are called in. Even if it's not customary in your area or if it's a "no gifts" party, close friends and family often do choose to give an engagement present. If so, they should present their gifts to the couple at a time and place other than the engagement party. An engagement gift shouldn't be expensive or elaborate. One popular idea is anything that might help the couple start a collection, such as a cookbook or nice bottle of wine. Or, if the friend is close to the bride, the present would usually be something for her—a piece of jewelry, a small box of fine stationery, or perhaps lingerie if from a female friend or relative.

"NO GIFTS, PLEASE" (PLEASE COMPLY!)

Gifts are customarily expected for many events—especially at birthday and anniversary parties—but when honorees really don't want presents, their wishes should be respected. In the past, any reference to gifts on invitations was considered in poor taste, because guests were supposed to know the occasions when gifts were obligatory. But today, it's generally okay to mention "No gifts, please" on invitations—other than on wedding invitations. (The thinking is that a wedding invitation is so special and the custom of giving the couple a gift is so entrenched that even the mention of gifts slants the emphasis toward gift giving and away from the inviting.) But in light of the current gifts-for-everything craze, it's a courtesy to inform guests on any occasion other than a wedding when presents are not expected. The etiquette is to write "No gifts, please" at the bottom of the invitation or to tell invitees when inviting them in person or by phone.

Here's the big thing: When you receive an invitation with a "No gifts, please" request, take it seriously. Showing up with a present when asked not to would embarrass the hosts, the honoree, and other guests who, correctly, didn't bring anything. If you want to give a gift as a special token of affection, do so at another time.

✻

Wedding Gifts: How Late Is Too Late?

QUESTION: I've heard that you have until one year after the wedding to send the couple a gift. Is that true?

ANSWER: No. Gifts should be delivered as close to the wedding date as possible. Most guests actually send gifts *before* the wedding, although some send them shortly after the wedding date, as well. Gifts can be sent as soon as the wedding invitation arrives.

DISPELLING WEDDING MYTHS

Myth: Women guests and bridesmaids shouldn't wear black or white to a wedding.

New Attitude: In most cases, women *can* wear black or white to a wedding. If you choose white, don't wear anything even remotely bridal, so you don't compete with the bride's dress. With black, go for chic, not funereal. Consider the time of day and the formality of the wedding. Black is more suited to a formal evening wedding than an afternoon garden wedding, for example.

Myth: The bride and groom must have a receiving line.

New Attitude: It's not necessary to have a receiving line, but it *is* necessary for the bride and groom to greet *every* guest. If logistics or timing make a receiving line impractical, or if the couple prefer to do so, they can greet guests individually by visiting their tables. Clearly, this is easiest to accomplish when the wedding is small (with seventy-five guests or fewer).

Myth: The mother of the bride or groom shouldn't host a shower.

New Attitude: Sometimes it makes the most sense for an immediate family member to be shower host. It used to be seen as self-serving—but now friends and families may be so far-flung that it can often work best for a family member on either side to host a shower for a visiting bride.

Myth: Female attendants represent the bride; male attendants stand up for the groom.

New Attitude: Brides and grooms who want to honor a special person in their lives—be it a relative or a friend—may choose to have an "honor attendant" rather than bridesmaids or groomsmen. A man or a woman can serve as an honor attendant for the opposite sex. The duties are adapted accordingly; a man wouldn't help the bride get dressed, for example!

❧

Inviting Coworkers

QUESTION: Is it okay to invite some work friends to my wedding, but not the entire department?

ANSWER: Yes, if you're diplomatic. Coworkers you don't socialize with shouldn't expect an invitation, but let everyone know from the start that the guest list will be limited so no one is disappointed. Keep pre-wedding chatter to a minimum to prevent hurt feelings. If you're close to your boss, invite him. It's a courtesy that shows you value the relationship, and he'll appreciate the gesture.

DRAWING UP THE LIST

Limit by category. Prevent hurt feelings by dividing your guest list into categories and inviting only those in certain groups. For example, you might invite aunts and uncles but forgo cousins. If things are really tight, eliminate second-tier groupings wholesale, such as work associates with whom you've never socialized or friends from the health club. Stick to your categories without exception, and no one will have hurt feelings.

Cut out coworkers. When space is really at a premium, one option is to delete work associates entirely. This can reduce the list considerably, while also keeping the wedding more personal. Or, you might invite only your boss and your respective assistants. Other coworkers will understand that you had to keep it small.

Beware parental payback. Don't let your parents insist that they need to reciprocate for all the weddings they've been invited to in the past. Your wedding should not be a vehicle to help them fulfill their social obligations.

Include shower guests. Any guest who is invited to a shower must also be invited to the wedding, with a few exceptions, such as coworkers who are not invited to the wedding but who give an office shower. Be careful when drawing up your shower guest list of friends and relatives.

Talk to long-distance friends. Call and ask friends who live far away if they think they'll be able to make it. If not, that may free up some extra space. (An important note: Really close friends and relatives who say they can't attend should be sent an invitation anyway. Even though they won't make it to the wedding, there's a good chance that they would be hurt if no invitation arrived.)

❄

Cash Only

QUESTION: My fiancé and I are close to thirty and have been living together for the past two years. We don't need much in the way of traditional household items, but we're saving for a down payment on a house. Is there an appropriate way to let guests know that we'd prefer cash to dishes and sheets?

ANSWER: The most polite and effective way to tell people what you'd like is by word of mouth. It's a good idea for couples to tell their parents and attendants where they're registered or, as in your case, that cash is preferred. But keep in mind that it's a guest's prerogative to choose your gift and you shouldn't dictate what it should be. If you're asked directly, say: "We're saving for a down payment on a house, so if you'd like to give us a check that's how we'll use it. But whatever you decide will be terrific. Thank you for thinking of us." Cash presents are perfectly acceptable, provided the guest feels comfortable with the idea; some people just don't like to give money. That's why it's a good idea to set up a traditional registry, even if it contains only a few items, so guests have a sense of what things you do like and need.

NEW TRENDS IN WEDDING REGISTRIES

Honeymoon Registry

WHAT IS IT?

These registries, available through many travel companies and agents, allow guests to contribute money toward a couple's honeymoon trip.

IS A HONEYMOON REGISTRY APPROPRIATE?

Sure, but don't expect all guests to pony up. Some may be more comfortable selecting a traditional gift or giving cash. It's a good idea to set up another gift registry as well.

HOW DO I SPREAD THE WORD?

Informing guests of your registries is best done the old-fashioned way—via word of mouth. Wait until someone asks either you or one of your relatives or friends. Then, it's okay to say where you're registered. If someone asks you, a courteous response would include not only retailer names, but also an appreciative comment such as: "Whatever you choose would be special. Thanks for thinking of us!" Discreet links to registries on your wedding Web site are also fine. Be certain to work with a reputable travel company, and one that will notify you of any cash gifts and the donors.

Charity Registry

WHAT IS IT?

Couples who don't want gifts ask that guests make donations to a favorite charity or nonprofit agency instead.

IS A CHARITY REGISTRY APPROPRIATE?

Yes. This is a special way for couples, especially those with established households, to mark their union. It's perfectly appropriate, as long as you avoid political or highly controversial causes. Since some guests may still want to give you a traditional gift, select at least a few items on a retail registry as well. If someone chooses not to use the charity registry, by giving either a traditional gift or cash, be gracious and appreciative.

HOW DO I SPREAD THE WORD?
Some charities have formal registries; for others, you'll have to ask your guests to contact the organization directly. Give close family and friends the contact information for the charities you consider worthwhile and ask them to inform others when asked for gift suggestions. The organizations will notify you of donations made in your name.

SHOULD THANK-YOU NOTES STILL BE SENT, OR IS THAT THE RESPONSIBILITY OF THE CHARITY?
Always send a handwritten thank-you note to each and every guest that gives you a gift. Do it as soon as you possibly can.

Alternative Retailer Registry

WHAT IS IT?
This is a registry at a specialized store such as one that sells home improvement supplies, sporting goods, camping gear, or furniture.

IS AN ALTERNATIVE RETAILER REGISTRY APPROPRIATE?
Certainly. A wedding is a gift-giving occasion and there's nothing wrong with registering for items that you would like, even if they're not the stuff of traditional registries. Couples with established households, for instance, often prefer to register for items targeted to their hobbies or interests, and that's perfectly fine.

�֍

Thankless Task

QUESTION: I attended a wedding four months ago and gave the couple a check as a gift. The check was cashed, but four months have passed and still no thank-you note! Isn't that too long?

ANSWER: The most common complaint—by far—from wedding guests has to do with overdue thank-yous. When a guest goes through the effort of thoughtfully selecting and giving a gift and then nothing happens—sometimes for months—he begins to wonder! "Was the gift ever received? If it was, why hasn't a note been written?" Thank-you notes should be written promptly—at the very least, within three months of receipt of the gift. If you haven't received a note three months after the couple received your gift, it's okay to ask the bride, the groom, or one of their parents if the gift was received. With any luck, a gentle nudge will get your point across and you'll find out if the gift was received and appreciated.

DO'S AND DON'TS OF WEDDING
THANK-YOUS

This checklist will help brides and grooms sidestep common note-writing blunders and make thank-yous easier to write and more meaningful to receive:

Do personalize your notes, referring to the givers as well as their gifts.

Do be enthusiastic, but be realistic with the praise. Refrain from saying it's the best gift you've ever received unless you really mean it. Sincerity counts.

Do refer to the use you will make of money gifts. Mentioning the amount is optional.

Do remember that a gift should be acknowledged with the same courtesy and generous spirit in which it was given.

Don't send form letters or cards with printed messages and just your signature. Don't use email or post generic thank-yous on your Web site, unless you follow up soon with written notes.

Don't mention that you plan to return or exchange a gift or indicate dissatisfaction in any way.

Don't tailor the quality of your note to the perceived value of the gift. No one should receive a dashed-off, perfunctory note.

Don't include wedding photos or use photo cards if it will delay sending notes.

Don't use your lateness as an excuse not to write at all. Even if your first anniversary has passed, the gift giver still deserves your written thanks, not to mention an apology for the delay.

✿

"The Envelope, Please"

QUESTION: I just received an invitation to a good friend's wedding. How do I know if it's okay to bring my girlfriend?

ANSWER: The answer is on the envelope. If your girlfriend's name, or your name followed by "and Guest," is written on the envelope, she's invited. If the envelope (the outer one, the inner, or both) contains only your name, you'll be attending stag. Often, due to limited seating and tight budgets, couples don't have the luxury of inviting their single friends with guests. Absolutely respect their wishes. And be sure to RSVP promptly. If you and your girlfriend become engaged before the wedding, then you can let the bride and groom know, as then it would be good manners for them to include your fiancée.

THE WEDDING GUEST'S PLEDGE

Before the Wedding . . .

I will RSVP immediately. A quick response helps the bride and groom stay on top of their planning. Your "can't attend" is as important as your "can."

I will send a gift. Invited guests have an obligation to send a gift, whether they're attending or not. (There is an exception: You may forgo the gift if you receive an invitation to the wedding of someone you haven't spoken to or seen in several years.) When sending a gift, it's best to do so close to the time of the wedding, sometime between receiving the invitation and soon after the wedding. The idea that you may wait a whole year before sending a wedding gift is an urban myth.

During the Ceremony . . .

I will respect the sanctity of the occasion. Loud talking, greeting or mingling with friends, taking flash pictures, and leaving cell phones on can disrupt the ceremony. Keep quiet, and silence ringers and pagers.

I will participate in as much of the ceremony as my own religion and that of the ceremony permit. If a Mass or Holy Communion is offered and you choose not to participate, remain quietly in your seat. Otherwise, stand when others stand and sit when they sit. You don't have to kneel, or to recite prayers that are contrary to your own beliefs.

I will not show up at the ceremony and/or reception with a surprise guest, whether date, child, or other relative. Respect the intent of the bride, groom, and hosts. This means that the names on the invitation envelope are the people who are invited. That's it! No bullying to bring your "perfect" child or latest love.

At the Reception . . .

I will not grab the microphone to croon a favorite number, or broadcast stories or jokes, no matter how entertaining I believe myself to be. The bride or groom may ask you to make a toast. If they haven't, then don't. Another reminder: Leave some space on the dance floor for the bride and groom. Don't be a guest who hogs the dance space or who allows his children (if present) to monopolize the show.

I will not move place cards or switch tables at the reception. Instead, be cordial to whomever the bride and groom seat you with. And don't stand on ceremony and wait to be introduced. Do so yourself and add an explanation: "I'm Laurie's aunt from Hawaii" or "Jen and I were roommates in college."

I will be gracious and help other guests if they need it. It's thoughtful for men at a table to ask single women to dance at some point during the reception, and for anyone to offer to assist an older or infirm guest in any way, such as to help with a buffet meal.

When It's Time to Leave . . .

I will take the hint and go home. When it's time, it's time. You'll know, such as when the bride and groom have left for their honeymoon and the band has wound down.

I will not take the centerpiece. Unless, of course, the hosts encourage you to do so. Nor should you scoop up matchbooks or request that any part of your meal be put in a doggie bag to take home.

✤

"Why Aren't the Kids Invited?"

QUESTION: I want to have an adults-only wedding, but I'm worried about my sister-in-law insisting on bringing my three young nephews. What's the correct way to let her know that her children aren't invited to the wedding?

ANSWER: The decision whether or not to include children is yours and your fiancé's—and no one has the right to insist upon bringing uninvited children to a wedding. If you are truly planning an adults-only wedding, don't let your sister-in-law bully you into including your three nephews. When children are not invited, the proper way to communicate this is to write only the parents' names on the outer and inner envelopes on your invitations. Don't write "No children" on the invitations.

CHILDREN AND WEDDINGS

One of the most hotly debated issues in planning a wedding is whether or not to invite children. Some people feel that having children at a wedding can be an intrusion, or a distraction for guests intent on participating in and honoring a very grown-up ritual. Others can't imagine a wedding celebration without children. Here are some general guidelines on inviting children—and not inviting them—to wedding celebrations:

How to set limits when inviting children. One option is to draw the line by setting an age limit—inviting children ten and older, for example. Other ideas include inviting only the children of close family members and/or children of the wedding party, but this can get complicated. Either way, once you've made your decision, make no exceptions, since doing so will cause more hurt feelings than standing firm.

How to explain "adults only." Launch a proactive campaign to get the word out that your wedding will be an adult affair. Discuss the situation with friends and relatives. Ask them to help spread the word. You may even want to enclose a note to those friends and relatives who may be the most upset by your decision, explaining that costs, space, and/or the formality of the setting prevent you from including children. Unfortunately, some guests choose to ignore (or truly misunderstand) the polite omission of their children's names on the wedding invitation and write or call to tell you that they are bringing their children. You'll have to have a direct conversation with the parents. "I'm sorry, Jan, but we aren't having any children at the wedding. We won't be able to accommodate Susan and Kurt." If this results in an angry "Then I'm not coming either," so be it. The breach of etiquette is theirs, not yours. Be sensitive to and aware of the fact that excluding children may mean that some friends and family members may be unable to attend the wedding.

Making accommodations for children. If you decide to include children in the wedding festivities, you'll want to make the occasion special for them, too. Finding ways to keep them occupied can be great fun. Some brides and grooms set aside a "children's room" at the reception and staff it with babysitters and fill it with toys. Aim for a reasonable adult-to-child ratio so that parents will feel comfortable with the arrangements. You could have your floral designer create a piñata, filled with inexpensive toys. Or you could set up a designated children's table at the reception with coloring books and favors. Include some kid-friendly foods on the menu. One final option: Get the names and numbers of a few area babysitters. Then provide the information to out-of-town guests who may wish to hire a babysitter during the hours of the wedding celebration to watch their children—either at a relative's home or at the hotel where the family is staying.

15

In Sad Times

Email Empathy

QUESTION: I just learned that a friend's husband passed away. Is it okay to send her an email expressing my sympathy?

ANSWER: If you're sure that a friend uses email frequently, it's okay to send her an email in the days just after her loved one's death, since it's an immediate and non-intrusive way to show her that you're thinking of her. But be sure to follow up soon with a handwritten note. It would also be thoughtful to call her, and to attend the funeral or visitation if you are able.

THE LONG AND THE SHORT OF
CONDOLENCE NOTES

Condolence notes are too personal to follow a formula, but here are some simple guidelines:

Say what you feel. Expressing one genuine personal feeling that you had for the deceased is better than the most expensive and eloquent store-bought card.

Make it short and sweet. A comforting note is personal and not long. Those struggling with a loss shouldn't have to wade through long-winded condolences.

Don't dwell on the details of the death or illness. Focus on a positive aspect of the person and his life.

Don't say, "It was for the best," or, "It's a blessing in disguise." Chances are, your friend does not think that her loss is a good thing, and saying so is presumptuous and potentially upsetting.

Offer some specific way to help if you can. "I'd like to bring you dinner some night this week if you'd like" is thoughtful. A general "Please call me if I can do anything" is not as helpful—unless you're close and there's a good chance your friend will call.

Just do it. Sure, it's not easy to write. Yet, a condolence note can really be a kind boost for the griever.

Here are two condolence notes that set the right tone:

Dear Carole,

We were so sad to hear of Jack's death. If Keith or I can help by shopping, running errands, or doing anything else for you, I hope that you'll call us. In the meantime, you are in our thoughts and prayers.

With deepest sympathy,
Sheryl

Dear Mr. Bronson,

    Although words cannot take away your sadness at such a time, I still want you to know that you're in my thoughts and prayers.

    Your mother held a special place in our hearts for as long as we knew her. The countless hours she spent with our son Jordan will always be remembered, and we will miss her nurturing presence very much.

With deepest sympathy,
Elliot McManus

When a Friend Gets a
Difficult Diagnosis

QUESTION: I just learned that a friend has cancer. I'll be seeing her at a get-together next week. Should I mention it? What should I say?

ANSWER: Wait for her to broach the subject. She may still be working through her emotions about her diagnosis, and talking about it may upset her. If she brings it up, however, offer your support and lend an ear. If you know for sure that she's talking about her illness with others in general, it's okay to take the initiative: "I just heard about your diagnosis from Stephanie. You know I'm here for you, so please let me know whenever I can help."

BEST—AND WORST—THINGS TO SAY
TO A SICK PERSON

It's especially important to choose your words carefully when you're talking to someone who is ill and no doubt feeling especially vulnerable. Here are three things *not* to say:

1. "I know how you feel." Only the sick person knows how he feels.

2. "You're going to be fine." Unless you have a medical degree, you don't know the prognosis, let alone the outcome. This is especially inappropriate to say to someone who is terminally ill.

3. "It's not that bad." Again, don't presume to tell the person how he's feeling. This statement might reassure the speaker himself, but would be upsetting to someone who is, in fact, feeling pretty bad.

A better approach is to listen to what the sick person has to say. Then, rather than trying to talk him out of feeling poorly, accept and acknowledge the situation and his feelings about it. Letting him know that it's okay to feel as he does will be reassuring and will help him feel better emotionally, if not physically. Here are some examples of empathetic statements:

"It must be tough."
"You must be feeling pretty tied down."
"It must be frustrating for you to feel so helpless."
"I'm so sorry you feel awful!"

If a person's chances for recovery are slim, steer clear of remarks that sound overly optimistic or pessimistic. If you are visiting someone who attends your house of worship, or who is receptive to praying together, that is an appropriate and calming way to show your support.

One key thing: Don't ignore someone who is seriously or terminally ill. It can be very lonely for that person to feel as if he's been "dropped" by others. The better thing to do is to keep in touch. Take your cue from the ill person as to how much one-on-one contact he would like. Even if you realize that he prefers no visits or even phone calls, some cards or emails can be uplifting reminders that someone is thinking about him—and cares.

✻

Short and Sweet Visits

QUESTION: How long should a visitor stay when visiting someone who's sick?

ANSWER: Twenty minutes at the most, even if your friend urges you to stay. If other visitors arrive while you're there, leave even sooner, so they have a chance to visit the patient, too, without wearing him out.

FOUR DON'TS FOR HOSPITAL VISITORS

What not to do while visiting someone in the hospital:

Don't wear perfume. Illness and certain medications can make odors more intense or even nauseating.

Don't sit on the bed. While you may think it shows affection and concern, it may also cause the patient pain.

Don't exclude the patient from the conversation. If two or three of you are visiting at the same time, for example, don't get into a discussion of the meeting you are all going to later that day at the school or a discussion of something in the newspaper the patient may not have seen.

Don't overstay your welcome. Keep your visit brief and upbeat, so you leave the patient with energy for the all-important healing process. Plan to stay no more than twenty minutes, and stick to it.

Brights or Black?

QUESTION: When attending a funeral recently, I was startled to see a few women wearing brightly colored dresses. The cuts weren't inappropriate, but I'd always thought you were supposed to wear black or another somber color at a funeral. Are bright colors okay?

ANSWER: While you'll never go wrong with black, these days bright colors are considered appropriate if the clothing is in good taste and appropriate for the place where the funeral is being held. So, no loud Hawaiian shirt, please—unless it's a perfect remembrance of the deceased and fits in correctly at the funeral location.

WHAT TO WEAR TO A FUNERAL

It all comes down to respect and personal choice. Some people say that, to them, a funeral service is a celebration of the deceased person's life and therefore they wouldn't wear black. One woman told me that she donned a red dress for her best friend's funeral service because it was her pal's favorite color. The decision of what to wear should also factor in the location of the service and your best guess as to the expectations of the bereaved family. Are the observances being held in a place of worship, or are they consisting of a eulogy at a funeral home or other venue? Do you sense that bright colors would cause the mourning family even more concern that day? Do you wonder whether to wear a suit or a sporty shirt? When in doubt, go with conservative clothes and colors. If you've thought carefully about the choices and believe you're okay with going bright or casual or both, then go for it—respectfully, of course.

When There's Good News and Bad News

QUESTION: A friend just gave birth to twins, but one was stillborn. I want to extend my sympathy for the passing of one daughter while expressing my happiness for the arrival of the other. Should I send two separate notes?

ANSWER: This is a time to extend condolences as well as share happiness, and you can do both in one note. Let your friend know she's in your thoughts. Use your own words to express your joy at the safe arrival of one child and your sorrow about her loss. Avoid statements like "It's for the best." You could close your letter by offering to lend a hand with errands or housework.

HOW TO COMFORT, NOT OFFEND

People are often reluctant to approach people who've lost loved ones because they're afraid they'll say the wrong thing. Keep these suggestions in mind and it will be easier to offer grieving friends or family members the comfort they need:

DON'T SAY	SAY INSTEAD
"He's in a better place."	**"I'm so sorry about your loss."**

"Did he have life insurance?"

"He was such a family man."

"Call me if there's anything I can do."

"Can I bring you dinner tomorrow night?"

"It's God's will."

"She was an extraordinary person."

"I know how you feel."

"Please know that I'm thinking of you."

"Now you're the man of the house."

"Your father was an example for us all."

✳